THE SOCIAL SECURITY MONEY CODE

How to Choose the Right Time to Claim, Avoid Costly Medicare & Tax Mistakes, and Maximize Every Dollar of Retirement Income You've Earned

By

GARRETT MONROE

THE SOCIAL SECURITY ACTION PACK

As a way of saying thank you for your purchase, we're giving you **10 FREE companion resources** created exclusively for readers of *The Social Security Money Code.* These practical tools are designed to help you apply what you learn in the book, stay organized, and make more confident Social Security and Medicare decisions.

Here's what you'll get:

1. The Social Security Money Code Action Pack
2. Interactive Claiming Age Calculator
3. 10-Year Retirement Roadmap
4. Major Life Change Planning Checklist
5. Social Security & Medicare Quick Reference Guide
6. 12-Month Pre-Claiming Countdown
7. "Call SSA Like A Pro" Script Pack
8. Tax-Free Retirement Paycheck Blueprint
9. Free Government Benefits Beyond Social Security
10. Widow(er) First-90-Days Action Card

To download your bonuses, scan the QR code or go to:

MonroeMethod.com/social-security

TABLE OF CONTENTS

INTRODUCTION:

DON'T CLAIM SOCIAL SECURITY UNTIL YOU READ THIS

For 40 years or so, a piece of every paycheck you earned went into Social Security, faithfully building the benefit you've now earned. In other words, you've held up your end. Now, just as it's your turn to collect, you hit a problem: The system hands you a benefit, but not the instructions that go along with it. When you claim, how you claim, and how it collides with taxes and Medicare can swing your lifetime income by tens of thousands of dollars, and many of us make those calls blindly.

This book is designed to help you make those decisions with confidence instead of guesswork.

Why This Decision Matters

Social Security is money you earned. It's funded by the payroll taxes you paid over the course of a working lifetime, which means that these benefits belong to you as much as a pension does.

Many nearing retirement underestimate how much their choices affect the size of those checks. For instance, the timing of when you claim can influence your finances for decades. Claim at one age, and you lock in one amount, but claim at another, and the number can look very different. That single decision shapes every check that comes after it. It's kind of like setting the thermostat for your retirement income: Once you pick a setting, it stays there year after year. The choice can feel small in the moment, but it determines what lands in your account each month for the rest of your life.

Those timing differences add up. A modest gap in your monthly check stretched across 20 or 30 years of retirement can turn into a significant sum (we're talking about thousands of dollars over time here). The difference between a careful choice and a rushed one can equal the cost of a nice car, or even substantially more.

This is a decision you can get *right*. You just need to understand the rules before you make it.

The Manual You Should've Been Given

Social Security comes with a long list of rules, but almost no guidance on how to turn those rules into the right decisions for your situation. To be fair, the Social Security Administration is helpful in one way: It can tell you what the rules are. But it can't sit down with you and build a personal strategy, and it won't tell you which choice leaves you better off.

That gap is exactly where this guide comes in. You need a roadmap, written in plain language, that turns a pile of rules into choices you can actually make. Think of this book as a steady hand that points out which turns matter and which ones you can ignore.

None of these rules are beyond you, and by the last page, you'll know them well enough to make this decision with confidence.

The Money Code Framework

Everything in these pages is organized around four questions, and if you can answer those, you have a real plan. We call this the Money Code Framework. The point of all of it is simple: to help you collect the largest lifetime payout you can from the benefits you've already earned. It isn't complicated, and you don't need a finance degree to use it. Essentially, they're four simple checkpoints on the way to a confident decision:

1. **When should I claim?** The timing decision that shapes every future check
2. **How do I maximize household benefits?** Covers spouses, survivors, and the income you share
3. **How do I keep more of my money?** Centers on taxes and smart withdrawals that protect your check
4. **How do Medicare decisions affect my retirement income?** The healthcare aspect that affects your monthly cash flow

Keep these four questions in mind as you read through these pages, because every chapter ties back to one of them. When a new rule feels confusing, ask yourself which checkpoint it belongs to. That habit alone will help you stay grounded no matter how detailed things seem.

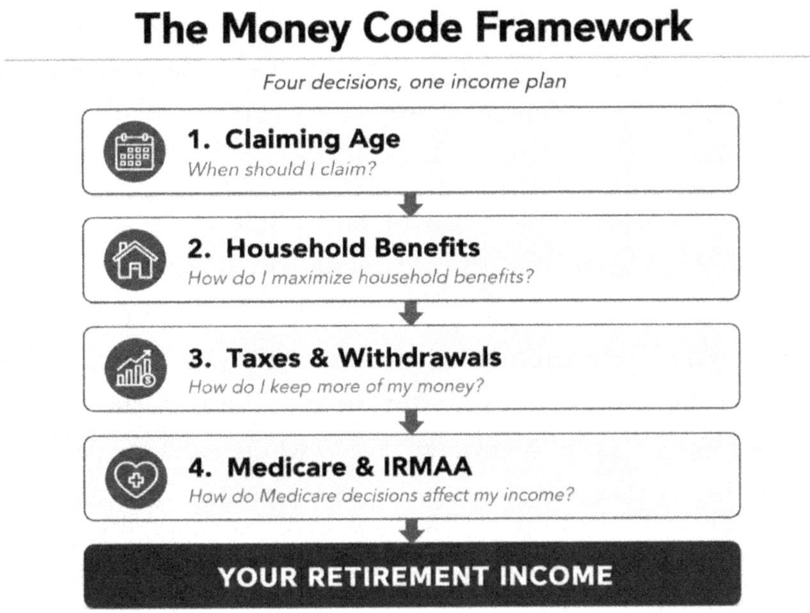

The four key questions at the heart of this book

Why So Many Smart People Get Social Security Wrong

Going about Social Security the wrong way generally comes from the way the system is built and the way advice tends to spread. The rules live in separate places, so they're easy to miss in their entirety. One office handles the claiming rules, another the tax treatment, and a third the Medicare timing. Nobody tells you how all these things fit together, and so you end up gathering pieces from different sources. It's easy to assume you have the full picture when you're really holding only one corner of it.

The advice you hear from friends and family is often conflicting, too. Your neighbor swears by claiming early, but your brother-in-law insists that you should wait until 70. Both are sharing what works or worked for *their* lives, which may look nothing like yours. Their health, savings, and family situations are different, so the answer that served them may steer you in the wrong direction.

These decisions also interact with each other, which means that a choice in one area changes the outcome in another. A claiming decision can raise your taxes. A withdrawal decision can push up your Medicare premium. In other words, pull one thread and the others move. This is why looking at any single decision by itself is generally a mistake, even when each piece seems reasonable on its own.

It's all too common to only discover how it all connects after the window to choose has already closed. And by that point, you're already locked in.

You get to do this differently by seeing the whole picture first.

How This Book Works

Here's the path we'll be following, in four simple parts:

1. **Part I** shows you how your claiming age affects lifetime income, and helps you find the filing approach that fits your situation.
2. **Part II** covers spousal, divorced-spouse, survivor, and work-related rules that can raise your household benefits.
3. **Part III** explains how taxes, withdrawals, and account decisions affect what you actually keep.

4. **Part IV** walks you through Medicare, the income surcharges that usually come as a surprise, and how healthcare costs fit into your strategy.
5. **Final Thoughts and Action Plan:** A full recap, along with one practical, One-Page Money Code Blueprint you can fill in, review, and update as your life progresses.

Before You Make Any Decisions

Social Security is too important to approach with guesswork, so let's set assumptions aside with an important reminder before we begin:

The goal is to match your choice to your life, your health, your savings, and the people who depend on you. The goal is *not* to claim as early as possible, or assume that waiting is always the better choice. The chapters ahead will help you weigh your options using facts rather than fear. You bring the details of your situation to the table, and I'll walk you through the rules in a way that's simple, concise, and easy to follow.

Let's begin with the decision that affects everything else: when to claim.

PART I:

YOUR FOUNDATION: THE CHOICE THAT SHAPES EVERY FUTURE CHECK

Long before taxes and Medicare enter the picture, one decision determines the starting point for your retirement income, and this is where you'll make it. These chapters help you find your real numbers and choose your claiming age intentionally rather than by accident. Go about this the right way, and the rest of your plan has a solid foundation to stand on.

CHAPTER 1:

THE CLAIMING DECISION YOU ONLY GET TO MAKE ONCE

Some decisions in life come with a do-over. You can change jobs, move to a new town, or rework a budget that isn't quite right. Claiming Social Security is different. For many, the choice you make is the one you live with and becomes the basis for every Social Security check you'll ever receive.

That might sound a bit daunting, but with a little planning and a clear view of your choices, this becomes one of the most rewarding decisions of your retirement years.

How Claiming Age Determines Your Lifetime Benefits

The easiest way to see why your claiming age matters is to watch it play out in real life, so before we get into the rules and the numbers, let's look at two people whose stories make the point click.

Two Similar Careers, Two Very Different Benefits

The numbers become much easier to understand when you see how they play out in real life.

> *Mike and David worked just down the road from each other and spent their careers in similar jobs, earned about the same paychecks, and paid into Social Security for roughly the same number of years. On paper, they looked almost identical. Then they reached the claiming window, and that's where their stories split.*
>
> *Mike turned 62 and figured that earlier was better. He filed right away without taking the time to compare his options, and his monthly check came in around $1,400. He was glad to have it. David looked at his situation differently. He spent a little time learning how the timing worked, and then waited until age 70 to claim. His monthly check came in at around $2,480. That's an enormous difference.*

Now stretch that gap across a long retirement by picturing both men living into their mid-80s. Over those years, the larger check could add up to roughly $100,000 or more in extra lifetime income for David. So while their careers had very closely matched one another, their retirements definitely didn't.

Why Claiming Age Matters

Mike skipped one important step: looking at his options before claiming. He made a permanent decision without comparing his choices first. That's the trap, and it catches otherwise careful people all the time.

Two things drove the gap between these men: timing and lack of planning. When they claimed made the biggest difference, and so did the actions leading up to that decision. Small, early choices created effects that followed each of them for decades.

The amount you lock in today matters, and this is exactly why your claiming age deserves your attention before you file anything. Throughout this chapter, you'll see why that one decision carries so much weight, and how a little planning helps protect the money you've already earned.

Once You Claim Social Security Benefits, You Can't Take Them Back

Claiming Social Security is less like flipping a switch and more like setting a course you'll hold for years, and knowing that up front makes the choice far less intimidating.

Social Security Is an Earned Benefit, Not a Handout

Remember, every paycheck you worked for helped fund these benefits, which makes them yours.

Your benefit is also adjusted for inflation, so it tends to keep pace with rising costs over the years. Few sources of retirement income offer that kind of built-in cost-of-living protection.

This money belongs to you, and whether you deserve it doesn't come into question. But understanding the rules helps you collect as much of it as possible.

Why Claiming Early Can Follow You for Life

Here's how the timing works in plain terms. Claim before your Full Retirement Age, and your monthly check is permanently reduced. Wait past that age, and your check grows through what are often called delayed retirement credits. These credits can be regarded, in simple terms, as a reward for waiting. For each year you hold off up to age 70, your future check gets bigger and stays bigger.

However, there *is* a narrow chance to undo a claim. If you change your mind within the first 12 months, you can withdraw your application, but you generally have to pay back what you received. After that short window closes, the opportunity to turn back time closes with it.

That's why the word *permanent* matters so much. A reduced check at 62 doesn't jump back to a larger amount later. It stays reduced in perpetuity.

How Claiming Early Affects Spouses & Survivors

It's crucial to remember that your claiming choice doesn't just affect you, but it also shapes the survivor protection you leave behind for your spouse.

When one partner passes away, the surviving spouse generally keeps the larger of the two checks. So if you claim early and lock in a smaller amount, you may also be locking in a smaller benefit for the person who outlives you.

We'll cover survivor benefits in detail in Chapter 7. For now, keep this top of mind: The size of your check today can echo through your household for decades. Treat this as an intentional decision that you make once, *after* looking at the numbers. But now we need to look at where people most often leave money behind.

Here's Where Social Security Money Gets Left on the Table

Lost benefits rarely vanish in dramatic ways. Instead, they slip away through a handful of common oversights, and all of them are easy to avoid once you know where to find them. Let's take a close look at the spots where money is most often left behind.

The #1 Mistake Retirees Make When Filing

Most of the money lost in Social Security is lost to a single, very human mistake: filing before running the numbers.

On the surface, it seems like a sensible decision. The money is available, so why wait? But assuming that earlier is automatically better is the most common and most expensive mistake that's made at the claiming window.

Remember Mike, who filed without comparing what claiming at 62, Full Retirement Age, or 70 would mean for him? That one skipped step cost his household a large sum over time.

Running the numbers simply means looking at your own benefit estimates side by side before you commit, no finance degree needed. We'll cover exactly how to do that in the next chapter.

Why Your Spouse's Benefit Matters

Another place money slips away is when couples make claiming decisions one at a time instead of as part of a coordinated strategy. This is significant because your timing can shape spousal benefits while you're both alive as well as survivor protection after one of you is gone. The timeframe you choose extends far beyond just your own check.

Imagine a married couple with one spouse earning considerably more than the other. If the higher earner claims early to get a check sooner, it may shrink the very benefit that protects the spouse later on. That single decision can influence your retirement together *and* the survivor's retirement afterward.

That's the part of Social Security many couples overlook: Your decisions are connected, because it's two checks, but one shared plan.

The Hidden Bite of Taxes & Medicare

Your claiming decision also ties into your taxes and your Medicare premiums in ways that are often unexpected.

A larger income from claiming can affect how much of your benefit is taxed, and it can also influence certain Medicare costs tied to your income. These pieces are connected, even though they sit in different offices and different chapters.

We'll tackle taxes, withdrawals, and Medicare in their respective chapters, and you'll see how each one ties back to the timing choice you make. For now, just take a mental note that these things work together, whether you initially realize it or not.

By now, it should be completely clear that claiming Social Security isn't a simple yes-or-no decision; it's a methodical choice that touches nearly every part of your retirement. The next question we'll explore is where to turn for guidance.

Who Should You Trust?

The right help is out there, but no one else can make this decision for you, and there are limits to what outside help can do for you. Understanding where guidance ends and your judgment begins is the key to getting it right.

What the SSA Can & Can't Do

The Social Security Administration is genuinely helpful, but there are limits you should plan around.

As mentioned earlier, the agency can explain the rules clearly. It can also tell you how much a benefit will be at a given age and process your application once you decide. What it generally can't do is build a personal strategy for you or tell you which choice leaves your household better off.

There's a real difference between someone who explains the rules and someone who helps you choose. The agency handles the rules, but it all comes down to you in the end.

You may also notice that answers can vary depending on who you reach out to. Two conversations with the SSA can sound surprisingly different, even when both representatives are following the same rules. This is because these reps simply aren't in the business of personal planning, and they aren't privy to the full picture of your life, your savings, or the people who depend on you.

Why Personal Planning Matters

No one knows your financial situation better than you do, and that's exactly why you need a framework rather than a single piece of advice. With a clear way to weigh your options, you stop relying on luck or on whomever happens to answer the phone.

The final decision belongs to you, but it should *never* feel like a guess. This guide is designed to help you understand your options, evaluate them clearly, and choose the path that best fits your retirement. And it all begins with your own numbers.

CHAPTER 2:

WHAT WILL YOU REALLY RECEIVE?

Two people of the same age, sitting at the same kitchen table, and both are certain that they know what their Social Security check will be. One's basing it on a figure in a letter from years ago, and the other heard a number from a friend who filed last spring. But neither has looked at an actual earnings record, and both are about to make a permanent decision based on a guess.

Before you decide when to claim, you need to know what you're actually working with, and that starts with one real number, pulled from your own record rather than a fuzzy memory or what a colleague told you.

Stop Guessing: Find Your Real Social Security Benefit

Before you pick a claiming age, you need one honest figure to build on. First clear out the guesses, then find the number that actually belongs to you.

Start with Your Real Numbers

Start with the facts. The only number worth planning around is the one pulled straight from your own earnings record, the year-by-year history of what you actually made and what was reported on your behalf. That record is personal to you, it reflects your real working life, and it's the base every claiming decision rests on.

The 3 Numbers That Can Change Your Retirement

You just need three figures to make a confident decision, and all of them come from your own record.

1. **Your age-62 number**: The smallest monthly check and the earliest you can claim retirement benefits
2. **Your Full Retirement Age number**: Your baseline, and the amount you receive if you claim at the age the system treats as your full retirement point
3. **Your age-70 number**: The largest monthly check, because benefit increases stop after this point

Write these three numbers down some place where you'll actually find them later. Keep them on one sheet of paper or in a note on your phone. We'll return to them repeatedly as you work through this decision.

Once you have those three figures from your own record, you've traded guesswork for facts. That's the first real step toward a decision you can trust, so now let's look at how the system comes up with those numbers in the first place.

How Social Security Actually Calculates Your Benefit

The math behind your check sounds complicated, but the core is simple: The system looks at your whole working life and pulls out your best earning years. Understand that, and the rest falls into place.

The Formula Behind Your Monthly Check

Social Security counts your highest 35 years of earnings, not your last 35 years or an average of everything. It reaches across your full career and pulls out the 35 years when you earned the most (adjusted for wage growth over time).

It's somewhat like a teacher grading your best 35 tests and tossing the rest aside; the strong years carry the weight. Those top years are added together and averaged, and that average becomes the basis for your monthly benefit.

Based on this alone, you can see how a long, steady work history tends to produce a stronger check. The more solid earning years you stack up, the better your best 35 look when the system puts them together.

How Missing Years Affect Your Benefit

If you worked fewer than 35 years, the system doesn't skip the missing time. Instead, it fills those empty slots with zeros.

Say you worked 31 years and took four years off to raise a family or care for a parent. The formula still wants 35 years, so it plugs in four zeros to complete the set. Those zeros drag your average down, which drags your check down with it.

The upside here is that those zeros aren't permanent if you're still working. Every year you keep earning gives you a chance to replace a zero, or a weak early-career year, with a stronger one.

> *Linda worked 33 years and had two zeros in her calculation. She stayed on the job for two more years, each at a solid salary. Those years filled the last two empty slots, and her monthly benefit climbed by roughly $40. That might not sound significant, but over a long retirement, that small bump turns into substantial money.*

This is what people online call the 35-year recalculation. Every year you keep working gives you another opportunity to strengthen the formula behind your benefit.

Why Full Retirement Changes the Rules

Once the system settles on your average, it sets your baseline benefit at your Full Retirement Age, or FRA. Think of FRA as the system's default setting, the point where you receive your full calculated amount with no bonus and no penalty.

Full Retirement Age by Birth Year

Your full retirement age depends on the year you were born.

Birth year	Full retirement age
1943–1954	66
1955	66 + 2 months
1956	66 + 4 months
1957	66 + 6 months
1958	66 + 8 months
1959	66 + 10 months
1960 or later	67

Anyone born in 1960 or later reaches full retirement age at 67.

FRA generally falls between 66 and 67, depending on the year you were born. Your birth year alone sets your exact full retirement point.

Claim before that age, and the system reduces your monthly amount for each month you claim early, because you'll likely collect more checks over your lifetime. Claim at 62, the earliest point, and your check can be cut by about 30% compared with your baseline.

Wait past your Full Retirement Age, and the *opposite* happens. Your check grows for each month you delay, all the way to age 70. These delayed retirement credits work as though they're interest on your patience, adding roughly 8% more per year you wait. After 70, the growth stops, so there's no reward for waiting longer than that.

Remember this: Your Full Retirement Age is the anchor. Every claiming decision is measured against it, either as a reduction for going early or a bonus for waiting. Find your birth year, confirm your full retirement point, and you'll know exactly what those three numbers on your sheet are telling you.

How Your Benefit Grows From 62 to 70

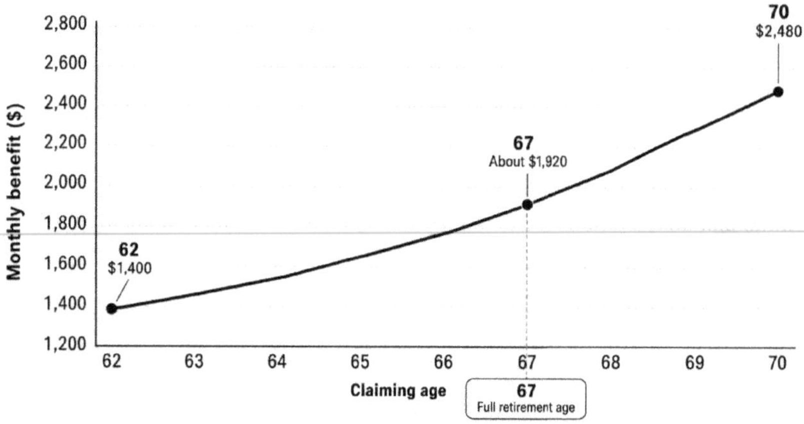

For this example worker, waiting from 62 to 70 raises the monthly benefit from $1,400 to $2,480.

Reading Your SSA Statement Like a Retirement Planner

Your real numbers live in one place, and you can access them yourself fairly quickly. Your own statement holds the *real* figures, and learning to read it puts you in complete control.

The Most Important Retirement Document You Could Be Ignoring

Your Social Security statement is the single most useful retirement document you have, and countless people never even open it. It shows your estimated benefits at different ages, and it lists your year-by-year earnings history.

That earnings history is the raw material for your entire benefit. If it's correct, your estimates are reliable, but if it's wrong, every number that follows is, too, so this one document deserves a careful look.

How to Create and Access Your SSA Account

Accessing your statement is easier than you might expect. You just set up a free personal account at ssa.gov, the official Social Security website. The process is a lot like setting up online access to your bank.

You'll verify your identity by answering a few questions only you should know the responses to, and then your statement is available whenever you want it. Once your account is active, you can check your numbers from your couch, no phone calls or office visits required.

If you'd rather not do it online, you can still receive a paper statement by mail. Either way, the goal is the same: to get your hands on your real figures so you're working from facts.

What to Check Before You Trust the Numbers

Once you're looking at your statement, don't just glance at the benefit estimates. Go straight to your earnings history and read it year by year.

Check three things in particular:

1. **Your earnings history:** Does each year roughly match what you actually earned?
2. **Missing years:** Do any working years show zero or a blank even though you know you had income?
3. **Obvious errors:** Does any year look far too low or otherwise clearly wrong?

If everything lines up, your estimates rest on solid ground and you can plan with confidence. If something looks off, look at that as a good thing; you've caught a problem early while there's still time to fix it. Speaking of which, let's examine some unassuming errors that might be lurking without your knowledge.

Hidden Problems That Can Shrink Your Check

Even a careful record can hide a few expensive gaps, shaving money off your benefit and often going unnoticed for years. But most of these can be fixed once you know where to find them.

The Missing Earnings Problem

Your benefit is only as accurate as your earnings record, so if a year of wages is missing or recorded too low, your checks will reflect that gap.

These mistakes happen more often than most think: An employer reports your wages under the wrong number, a name change after marriage scrambles your record, or a year simply never gets posted. The system is huge, and therefore it's quite easy for records to slip.

> *Robert noticed that one of his early working years showed zero earnings, even though he remembered working full-time that year. He dug out an old tax return, took it to Social Security, and got the record corrected. That simple fix raised his eventual benefit, all because he took the time to check.*

Keep old tax returns and W-2 forms when you can, because they're your proof if a year ever looks wrong. The sooner you spot a gap, the easier it is to correct.

How Self-Employment Income Affects Your Benefit

If you've ever worked for yourself, this one is worth a close examination. When you're self-employed, you report your own income and pay the tax that funds your future benefits.

Some self-employed people report as little income as they can in an effort to try and cut their tax bill. It feels like a boon at tax time, but the trade-off shows up years later as a smaller Social Security check than they'd been expecting.

The income you report as a self-employed worker is what counts toward your benefit. As long as you report your true earnings, you'll pay a bit more now but will also build a stronger check for life.

Maria ran her own shop for 15 years and reported modest income to keep taxes low. When she finally checked her statement near retirement, those lean reporting years had pulled her benefit well below what she'd expected, and there was no going back to redo it. If you're self-employed and still working, you need to weigh today's tax savings against the lifetime benefit you're building.

How Government Pension Rules Changed in 2025

If part of your career was in a job that didn't pay into Social Security (e.g., certain government, teaching, or public-service work), one more thing is worth knowing: There are two rules that previously reduced benefits for people who also received a pension from work not covered by Social Security. The first was the Windfall Elimination Provision, or WEP. It reduced the Social Security benefit of someone who earned a pension from work in which they didn't pay Social Security taxes. The second was the Government Pension Offset, or GPO, which reduced the spousal or survivor benefit of a person in that same situation.

But both of these rules are now gone. In January 2025, the Social Security Fairness Act was signed into law, and it repealed both WEP and GPO. People who've spent part of their careers in public service are no longer subject to these reductions, and the Social Security Administration has been restoring benefits and paying amounts retroactive to January 2024.

Because this change is recent, you may still run into older guides, forum posts, or headlines that describe WEP and GPO as active rules that shrink your benefit, but this is no longer the case. If a source still treats these provisions as in force, it's out of date.

So if you or your spouse worked in public service and earned a pension, the repeal may have raised your benefit or made you newly eligible for one. It's worth confirming directly with Social Security that your record reflects the change. Pull your statement, check your numbers, and ask about your situation under the current rules.

With your age-62, Full Retirement Age, and age-70 benefit amounts recorded; your earnings history confirmed; and any hidden problems flagged, you now have something that most others don't: a clear picture of what you've *actually* earned. That picture makes the next important decision possible, which is when to claim.

CHAPTER 3:

WHEN TO CLAIM: THE $100,000 SOCIAL SECURITY QUESTION

No single retirement choice moves more money than this one, and it has nothing to do with which fund you pick or how you invest. Time it well and you can add tens of thousands of dollars to your lifetime income. Time it poorly and you hand that same amount back without ever seeing the bill. People will spend an entire weekend hunting for a better mortgage rate, then make this much more significant decision in an afternoon. It deserves more careful attention than that, but all it really comes down to is taking your own numbers and making sense of them so that your decision is an educated one.

Now it's time to see what those three numbers are really telling you. By the end of this chapter, you'll be able to easily weigh your three numbers and choose your game plan with confidence.

The Choice That Shapes Every Check

Think back to the three numbers you wrote down: your age-62 amount, your FRA amount, and your age-70 amount. The gap between the smallest and the largest is usually fairly wide. For many people, the age-70 check is more than *75% larger* than the age-62 check. That's the difference between two very distinct lifestyles, one that's less abundant and one that's more comfortable. Picture what that could mean in ordinary life: The smaller check might cover the basics with little room left over, while the larger one might cover those same basics and still leave money for travel, gifts to grandchildren, or even just a cushion that helps you sleep better at night.

Why the "Best Age" to Claim Doesn't Exist

The best age to claim depends entirely on the person making the decision. (If an ideal age across the board *did* exist, this chapter would be much shorter.)

The right age for you depends on your health, savings, income needs, and the people who depend on you. A newspaper headline can't know any of that, nor can the neighbor accurately deduce that their situation is the same as yours. There's no formula that works equally well for every retiree because no two retirements unfold the same way. So instead of chasing a universal answer, you need to find *your* answer, the one that matches *your* numbers and goals. The whole decision becomes clearer the moment you stop borrowing other people's reasoning and start looking at your own figures. So let's build that comparison, starting with the case for going early versus waiting.

Should You Claim Early? Or Wait?

Both choices have real merit. Anyone who says that claiming early is always foolish or that waiting is always smart is skipping the part that matters most: examining everything in a way that's relevant to the specific situation.

When Claiming Early Makes Sense

As mentioned previously, claiming early means a permanently smaller monthly check, but for plenty of people, it's actually the sensible move.

First off, your health matters more than anything. If your health is fragile or your family history indicates that you may have a shorter lifespan, waiting years for a bigger check makes little sense because the reality is that you may not be around to collect it. Money in hand now can matter more than a larger amount you might never fully receive; this is simple math with a human face. Keeping your own health picture at the forefront of your decision is one of the wisest things you can do here.

Immediate income need is the next honest reason. If you're out of work at 63, your savings are thin, and the bills are real, claiming early can be the difference between steady ground and a scramble. Remember, a smaller check that arrives on time beats a larger one that shows up after you're gone. If you delay without a bridge, you may end up running up credit card balances or draining an emergency fund, whereas a consistent check now protects everything else you've built.

Lifestyle matters as well. Maybe you want to travel, help a grandchild with their tuition, or just enjoy your healthiest years while you still have them. There's nothing reckless about choosing income now to live your life the way you want to.

Sometimes waiting just doesn't fit the circumstances. If you have no other income and no interest in keeping work going, holding out until 70 may not be realistic. The best plan on paper is useless if you can't live on it in the meantime.

When Waiting Until 70 Can Increase Your Monthly Social Security Income

Now for the other perspective. Waiting can be a powerful way to raise your income for the rest of your years, and the engine that powers that decision is delayed retirement credits.

As noted already, for each year you wait past your Full Retirement Age, up to 70, your future check grows by about 8% according to the Social Security Administration's guidance on delayed retirement credits. There's no investment that gives you a guaranteed raise like that without market risk. Imagine a savings account that promised an 8% increase every year you left it alone, with zero chance of loss; you'd probably tell every friend you have. That's essentially what waiting offers, backed by the federal government rather than the stock market.

Another advantage is that your Social Security check rises with inflation each year. A larger starting check means that every future cost-of-living increase is calculated on a bigger number, so the gap between waiting and claiming early tends to *grow* over time, not shrink.

Longevity is where waiting really pays off. If you come from a family with a strong line of longevity and your health is good, those extra years of larger checks can add up in your favor. The longer you live, the more waiting rewards you. It's essentially insurance against living a very long time. If you reach 90 and beyond, that larger monthly check helps keep your finances steady during years when other savings may be running thin. It's a safeguard for your future self.

For married couples, there's one more advantage worth noting. When the higher earner waits and locks in a larger check, that amount can become the survivor benefit. It can support a surviving spouse for years after the first partner dies. We'll spend some more time explaining those survivor rules in detail later.

Understanding the Trade-Off Between Earlier & Larger Benefits

When weighing these options, it helps to see the trade-off underneath them. In short, claiming early gives you more years of payments, just smaller ones. Waiting gives you fewer years of payments, but each one is larger.

That's the heart of it. Do you want more checks or bigger checks? The right answer depends on your cash flow needs today and how long you expect to be collecting. Keep that question in mind as we look at the numbers. It keeps the decision simple and human, even when the figures start piling up.

Run the Numbers Before You File

Not a rough guess or a gut feeling, but a real comparison using your own figures. It's much simpler than it sounds, and it changes everything.

Understanding Your Break-Even Age

The most useful tool for this is the break-even age, which is the age at which the total money from waiting catches up to the total money from claiming early.

Let's use the example of two runners. The early claimer gets a head start and collects checks years before the person who waits. The person who waits starts later but runs faster with a bigger check each month. At some point, the faster runner catches up and passes the one who started early. That catch-up point is your break-even age. Slowly, the bigger checks close the gap, and for many, that catch-up point lands somewhere in the late 70s to early 80s. It's a useful way of looking at this because it frames the choice so clearly. If you expect to stay in the race well past that point, the faster runner is the better bet. If your race is likely to be shorter, the head start matters more.

But ultimately, you need to use break-even as a guide and not a crystal ball, because it can't tell you exactly how long you'll live.

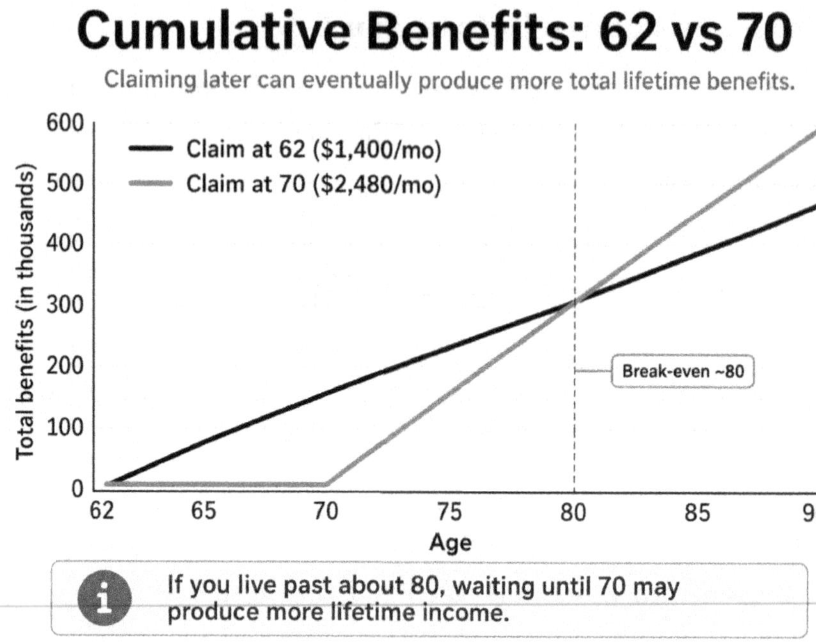

The lifetime totals reveal the trade-off. Waiting rewards longevity, while claiming early can produce more lifetime income if retirement is unexpectedly short. That's why there's no "one right answer" for when to claim. It depends on *you.*

Life Expectancy Is the Key Variable

While you can't know your exact lifespan, you can make a thoughtful estimate. Look at your own health and your family history honestly. Did your parents and grandparents live into their 90s, or did heart trouble cut things short? That pattern isn't a definitive answer, but an educated clue worth weighing. Your own lifestyle adds to the picture, too. Regular physical activity and good relationships with your doctors increase the possibility of living longer, as do maintaining a steady weight and looking after yourself in a general sense.

If you have solid reason to expect a long life, waiting tilts the odds in your favor because you'll likely move well past your break-even age and collect those larger checks for years. If your health and history point the other way, claiming earlier deserves a serious rethink.

Estimate your break-even age, compare it honestly with how long you expect to live, and let that become the starting point for your decision. Then bring your savings, spouse, and income needs into consideration, and things will become a lot clearer.

How the Right Choice Varies From Person to Person

Numbers come alive when you attach them to real people. Let's compare four retirees facing the same question, each arriving at a different answer that fits their life.

Single Retiree with Limited Savings

> *Carol is 62, single, and has recently been laid off. Her savings are modest, and finding new work at her age has been a challenge, but the bills don't take a break while she figures things out.*
>
> *For her situation, claiming early makes sense. A smaller check that starts now gives her steady ground and keeps her from draining what little savings she has. The bigger check at 70 is appealing in theory, but she has no realistic way to bridge those eight years without income. Carol also gains something harder to measure, which is*

peace of mind. With a reliable check arriving each month, she can stop scrambling and start planning.

Married Couple Planning Together

Tom and Susan are both 64 and planning their futures as a team. Tom earned considerably more over his career, so his check is the larger of the two. They have enough savings to be flexible.

The smart move for them is a blended one. Susan, the lower earner, claims earlier to bring in some income, while Tom, the higher earner, waits as long as he can to grow his check. That larger amount does double duty: It lifts their income while they're both alive, and becomes the survivor benefit that protects whoever lives longer.

Healthy Retiree with Longevity on His Side

George is 66, in excellent health, and his parents both lived into their 90s. He has solid savings and a part-time income he enjoys.

George is the textbook case for waiting. With likely a long life ahead and enough money to live on in the meantime, delaying to 70 stacks the odds in his favor. He'll probably collect those larger checks well past his break-even age, turning his patience into a substantial lifetime gain. His part-time income also makes the wait comfortable rather than stressful. He covers his bills with work he likes while his future check keeps growing in the background.

Retiree Facing Health Challenges

Diane is 63 and managing a serious health condition. Her doctors are direct with her, and her family history doesn't give her the best odds.

For her, waiting until 70 probably won't pay off. Chances are strong that she may not live long enough to reach her break-even age, which means that the larger check would never have time to catch up. Claiming earlier lets her use the money she earned while she still can. Though it's not necessarily the happiest of projections, this is Diane's most practical move.

Which Claiming Age Fits Different Retirement Situations?

It helps to see these patterns side by side, so the table below offers a quick read on how different situations tend to line up with each claiming age. A word of caution, though: Treat it as a conversation starter rather than a final verdict.

How Different Situations Can Affect Your Best Claiming Age

A quick, side-by-side guide to whether age 62, Full Retirement Age, or age 70 is the best option.

Situation	Age 62	FRA	Age 70
Poor Health	Often Strong	Possible	Usually Less Sensible
Average Health	Depends	Strong	Strong
Excellent Health	Usually Weaker	Strong	Often Strongest
Low Savings	Often Sensible	Depends	Sometimes Difficult
High Savings	Optional	Strong	Often Strongest
Married High Earner	Usually Weaker	Strong	Often Strongest

This is a general guide. The strongest claiming choice depends on your health, savings, marital situation, and expected longevity.

Read the table by finding the row that sounds most like you. If you're in excellent health with high savings, your row points pretty clearly toward waiting. If your health is poor or your savings are thin, the earlier columns start to make more sense.

You may also find that two rows describe you at once. A married high earner with excellent health sees the same answer from both rows, which makes the choice easier. When two rows pull in different directions, that's your cue to look more carefully at your own numbers and decide which factor matters more in your life.

Could Social Security Really Run Out of Money?

For many people, fear about the program's future pushes them toward claiming early, so it's a good idea to replace that fear with a clearer picture.

What Social Security Insolvency Could Mean for Future Benefits

The worry is understandable. Headlines warn that Social Security is running out of money, and so it's natural to wonder whether your benefits will still be there when the time comes.

But what those headlines are actually saying is that the program holds reserve funds that help pay benefits. Current projections suggest that those reserves could be depleted in the years ahead if lawmakers make no changes. The word "insolvency" sounds frightening, but it doesn't mean that the money stops.

Even if the reserves run low, payroll taxes from today's workers keep coming in. According to the Social Security Board of Trustees, those taxes alone are projected to cover roughly three-quarters of scheduled benefits. So the realistic concern is a possible future reduction, not a disappearance, and that's a long way from the doomsday version the headlines sell.

None of this is a guarantee about future policy, but it *is* the picture that current law supports. Let's use the example of a household that spends a bit more than it earns for a while. The income doesn't vanish, but it does mean that cuts, adjustments, or both may be needed later.

Why Claiming Early Because of Fear Can Be a Costly Mistake

The thinking goes, *I'd better grab my money before it vanishes.* But as noted above, the money *isn't* vanishing, and that fear-based move locks in a permanently smaller check.

There's a real difference between reduced benefits and no benefits, or in other words, a program that pays most of what was promised isn't the same thing as one that pays nothing. Building a permanent decision around the worst rumor instead of the more realistic projection usually costs people money. Plan with the law you have, not the rumor you fear.

How to Make a Smart Decision When the Future Is Uncertain

All of this means handling uncertainty rationally and calmly. Accept that laws and projections can shift, then focus on what you can actually control.

You control your numbers, health estimate, savings, and timing. Build your claiming strategy around your personal situation using the break-even thinking we just covered. That gives you something solid to stand on regardless of what lawmakers do. It also keeps you from getting misled and terrified by sensationalistic news cycles.

It's your responsibility to stay informed. As laws and projections change, revisit your assumptions and adjust them as needed. Your plan is never finished; you keep it current as the facts change.

PART I

WRAP-UP

You've now worked through the first and most important question in the Money Code Framework: *When should I claim?* But before moving on, let's tighten up the key points.

The Core Ideas

Your claiming age sets the size of every future Social Security check you receive. The best claiming age depends on your situation, not on a universal rule or someone else's story. And your decision should rest on your own numbers, not on fear or headlines.

Common Claiming Mistakes

Keep an eye out for the three traps that catch otherwise careful people most often:

- Claiming without first checking your real benefit estimates
- Claiming early out of fear that Social Security will disappear
- Skipping the break-even comparison that makes the trade-off clear

Your Part I Action Plan

Steps to take before you turn the page:

1. Create or verify your account at ssa.gov
2. Record your age-62, Full Retirement Age, and age-70 benefit estimates
3. Identify your tentative claiming age and the reasons behind it
4. Note any earnings-record errors to follow up on. If you or your spouse earned a pension from public-sector work, confirm that your benefit reflects the 2025 repeal of WEP and GPO.

Armed with clarity in terms of when to claim, the next piece is strategy at home. Part II shifts us into the benefits that can stretch across an entire household, starting with how two people can coordinate two separate benefits.

PART II:

MAXIMIZE EVERY SOCIAL SECURITY DOLLAR

Spouses, ex-spouses, survivors, and work income all open doors to money that so many of us never claim. These chapters show you how to find every dollar your household is owed, and time it so that none of it slips away needlessly.

CHAPTER 4:

TURNING TWO BENEFITS INTO ONE HOUSEHOLD STRATEGY

Most married couples make two separate Social Security decisions, and that's their first mistake. True, you have two checks, but one household lives on what those checks add up to, and you're far better off planning as a team rather than two people filling out separate forms. Done right, coordinating your timing can add tens of thousands of dollars to your lifetime income and protect whoever lives longer.

The upshot here is that coordinating as a couple isn't complicated once you see it clearly. It simply means looking at the two of you as a team instead of separate individuals.

The Cost of Treating Social Security as Two Separate Decisions

When two people share a retirement, they also share the consequences of each claiming decision. Considering each benefit in isolation can make a perfectly reasonable choice seem like the right one, even when it reduces the income the household will eventually depend on.

Why Two Smart Filing Decisions Can Still Cost a Couple Money

Frank and Joan are both 63. Frank earned more over his career, so his FRA check would be about $2,400, while Joan's would be about $1,200.

They each decide on their own. Frank wants his money sooner, so he claims early and locks in roughly $1,800. Joan does the same and locks in around $900. Both feel fine about it, and each feel that they've made a perfectly normal choice.

If Frank passes away first, which is statistically likely, Joan will step up to the larger of their two checks, which is Frank's. But because Frank claimed early, his check was locked in at a reduced amount, and that reduced amount is exactly what Joan will inherit as her survivor benefit. So the check she'll live on is permanently smaller than it would've been if Frank had waited. She may spend another 10 or 15 years on a survivor benefit that one early decision significantly shrank.

Nobody did anything reckless here; they simply planned as two individuals instead of one household. That's an oversight that can cost a couple many thousands of dollars over a long retirement.

Total Household Income Matters More Than Your Individual Benefit

Stop asking, "What's the best decision for me?", and flip the question to, "What's the best decision for *us*?" That's the mental shift that'll result in significant gains.

The number that matters most is your total household income, both while you're alive together *and* after one of you is gone. Your individual check is only one piece of that bigger picture. Plan around the household total, and the pieces start to fit in a way they never do when each of you goes it alone.

When you're planning your household budget, it's not as if you track one another's grocery money separately. You look at what comes in and what goes out as one shared pool, right? Your Social Security checks deserve the same treatment.

How Coordinated Claiming Can Increase Lifetime Benefits

Now let's replay Frank and Joan with a coordinated plan.

> *Joan, the lower earner, claims earlier to bring income into the house. Frank, the higher earner, waits as long as he comfortably can and lets his check grow. His larger check helps support them while they're both alive, and after he's gone, it becomes the survivor check that matters most.*
>
> *The difference during Joan's later years can be enormous. Instead of living on a reduced survivor check, she carries forward the larger amount Frank built by waiting.*

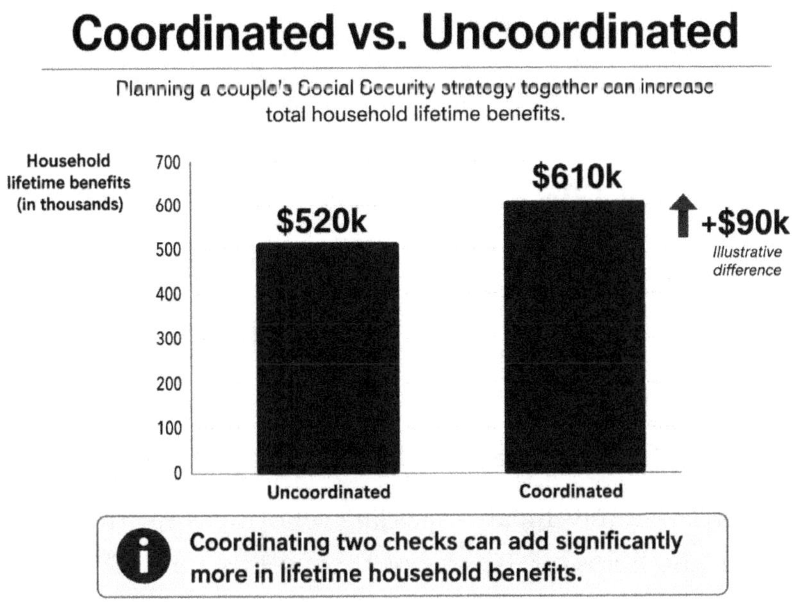

One coordinated decision, built around your household total, usually protects both of you better than two separate choices that accidentally work against each other. Next, we'll explore why one of your two checks carries far more weight than the other.

Why the Higher Earner's Claiming Age Matters More

In nearly every couple, one person tends to have earned more over the years. That higher earner's claiming decision carries extra weight, and once you understand why, you're in a much stronger position.

The higher earner has the larger benefit, so that person's timing pulls the bigger lever. When they wait, the household's biggest check grows, but when they claim early, the biggest check shrinks for good.

The lower earner's timing matters too, but there's simply less money riding on it. If you only have the energy to think hard about one decision, make it the higher earner's.

Who Should File First & Who Should Wait?

Once you start thinking like a household, the natural question is: *In what order should the two of us claim?* You don't have to file at the same time, and often, you shouldn't.

The Filing Order Question Every Couple Must Answer

Filing order simply means deciding who turns on their check first and who holds off. It's one of the most useful tools you have as a couple, because it allows you to bring in income now while still growing your most important check for later.

Sequence matters more than most couples realize. The right order gives you steady cash today and a larger protected check later. The wrong order, or no plan at all, often means that both benefits are smaller than they needed to be.

When Delaying Benefits Can Improve Household Income

Delaying works best for the higher earner's check, for the reasons noted above. Every year that check waits past FRA, it grows through delayed retirement credits, roughly that 8% annual boost mentioned earlier. It's basically a raise that the household locks in for life.

Of course, waiting has its downsides. While the higher earner holds off, that check isn't paying anything yet, so you need income from somewhere else in the meantime. That's exactly where filing order proves useful. The lower earner can claim first to help cover the gap while the bigger check keeps growing in the background.

The ideal balance? You want enough cash flow today to live comfortably, without claiming the higher earner's check so early that you shrink the income meant to protect you both later.

3 Common Claiming Strategies for Married Couples

Many couples land on one of three approaches. Find the one that sounds most like your situation:

> **The stagger:** *The lower earner claims earlier to bring income into the house, while the higher earner waits to build the largest possible check. This is the workhorse strategy for couples who want income now and stronger survivor protection later. The great thing about this is balance, but the negative aspect is that the higher earner needs patience, and the household itself needs the means to make waiting plausible.*
>
> **Both wait:** *If you have solid savings or other income to live on, both of you delay to grow both checks. While this ensures the largest possible monthly income later and strong protection for the survivor, it also means that you need enough money to bridge the early years comfortably, and not every couple has that option.*
>
> **Both claim earlier:** *When savings are thin, health is a concern, or you just need the income now, both of you claim sooner.*

> *This results in immediate cash flow and peace of mind, but also permanently smaller checks, including the survivor check. (But for some households, this is still the right call out of necessity).*

Having this crucial conversation can be worth more to your future than almost anything else in this guide.

CHAPTER 5:

BREAKING DOWN THE SPOUSAL BENEFIT: HOW COUPLES CAN MAKE THE RIGHT DECISIONS

The idea is simpler than it sounds. When one person earns far more than the other, the spouse with the smaller record may be able to claim a larger check based on their partner's work history instead of their own. In this chapter, we'll clear up all the confusion surrounding this benefit.

The Spousal Benefit That Can Increase Your Monthly Check

When a Spousal Benefit Can Increase Your Income

A spousal benefit lets the lower-earning partner collect a check based on the higher earner's record. This matters most when there's a wide gap between the two records. Maybe one of you stayed home for years, worked part-time, or simply earned far less in a lower-paying field. Whenever your spouse's benefit is much higher than yours, the spousal benefit deserves careful consideration.

Frequently, a couple will glance at the lower earner's statement, see a modest number, and assume that it's the whole story. They don't realize that a second option has been sitting there the entire time.

Who Actually Qualifies for a Spousal Benefit?

The rules here are quite lenient. You generally need to be married, and in most cases, the marriage must have lasted at least one year. But there's a timing issue that trips couples up constantly: Your spouse usually has to file for their own benefit before you can collect a spousal benefit on their record, though there are exceptions. The higher earner often needs to start their check first, and then the door opens for the lower earner to claim alongside it.

The most common misunderstanding is the belief that a low earner is stuck with their own small check, but that's not how it works. If you're married to someone with a much larger benefit, you may have the better option of waiting as long as the filing order lines up.

Should You Take Your Own Benefit or a Spousal Benefit?

This is fairly cut and dry: You compare two numbers and take the larger one.

First, look at your own benefit, the check built from your personal earnings record. Then look at the potential spousal benefit, the amount you could receive based on your spouse's record. Social Security doesn't stack these on top of each other. You receive the higher of the two, not both.

So compare before you claim. Pull both numbers, set them side by side, and see which wins.

> *Helen's own check would be about $700 a month. Her husband earned far more, so when she compares her own benefit with what she could draw on his record, the spousal option comes out noticeably higher. Once she looks, the answer is obvious, and that comparison is what the whole game is about.*

How Spousal Benefits Are Really Calculated

All you need here is a basic feel for how the spousal amount is set so that the figures on your statement stop looking mysterious.

Can You Really Receive Half of Your Spouse's Benefit?

You may have heard that a spousal benefit equals half of your spouse's check, but this is nuanced. At most, a spousal benefit can reach up to 50% of your spouse's full benefit, the amount they'd receive at their Full Retirement Age.

This is the part that's tricky. That "half" is measured against your spouse's full benefit, not the larger check they might get by waiting until 70. So if your spouse waits and grows their own check past their full amount, that delay doesn't also increase your spousal benefit. Your maximum is still tied to their full benefit figure.

Why Your Own Benefit Still Matters

Social Security looks at your own benefit first. If your spousal amount is larger, they top you up to that higher figure. You are not getting your own check plus a full spousal check. You are being brought up to the bigger of the two. So if your check is $700 and your spousal amount works out to about $1,200, you don't collect $1,900. Instead, your $700 is lifted to the $1,200 spousal level. The two pieces coordinate into one larger check, exactly as the system is designed to work.

The Rules That Catch Many Couples Off Guard

A lot of couples read about clever filing tactics online, with articles talking about claiming one benefit now and switching to another later. Many of those strategies no longer exist, and following old advice can send you straight into a bad mistake.

The reason comes down to something called deemed filing, which means that when you apply, Social Security treats you as claiming everything you're eligible for at that moment. You can't pick only the spousal benefit and let your own check grow on the side. When you file, you file for both, and you receive the larger one.

That rule killed off most of the old "restricted" strategies you may still see floating around, methods that let certain people claim one benefit while delaying another. But for the majority of today's retirees, this is no longer an option.

Many build a plan around advice that no longer applies, then feel blindsided when Social Security tells them that it can't be done. Save yourself that frustration by treating any "claim one, switch later" tip with caution and confirming the current rules.

Why Filing Early Can Permanently Reduce a Spousal Benefit

Timing shapes the size of the check, and the spousal benefit is no exception.

The Trade-Off Between Earlier Payments & Larger Spousal Benefits

Just like your own retirement check, remember that a spousal benefit shrinks if you claim it before your Full Retirement Age. Claim early, and you lock in a permanently smaller amount.

Claim the spousal benefit at 62, and instead of that full $1,200, you might receive something closer to $850. Wait until your FRA, and you collect the full spousal amount.

Why Full Retirement Age Determines Your Maximum Spousal Benefit

Your FRA is the point where the spousal benefit reaches its maximum of roughly half your spouse's full check. File before that age, and the amount is trimmed down month by month.

Just keep in mind that a spousal benefit doesn't grow past your Full Retirement Age, because the delayed retirement credits that reward waiting on your own check don't apply to spousal benefits. Clearly, there's no bonus for holding out beyond your full age on a spousal claim.

Should You Wait Longer to Claim a Spousal Benefit?

This decision is more straightforward than deciding when to claim your own retirement benefit. With a spousal benefit, waiting past Full Retirement Age earns you nothing extra, so there's no reason to delay beyond that point just to grow it.

The choice comes down to receiving income sooner or waiting until FRA for the full benefit. If you need the money sooner and the reduced check works for your situation, claiming early can still be the right call. If you can hold off until your full age, you preserve every dollar the spousal benefit offers. Compare those two scenarios against your household needs, and you'll know which path fits.

CHAPTER 6:

DIVORCED-SPOUSE BENEFITS EXPLAINED

If your marriage ended years ago, it's common to assume that Social Security closed that chapter when the divorce did. It often did not. A marriage that lasted for at least 10 years can still entitle you to a check based on your former spouse's record, sometimes a larger one than your own. Those years mattered for more than sentimental reasons, and they may be worth substantial money to you.

Understanding Divorced-Spouse Benefits

Social Security has a benefit built specifically for divorced people, and it's one of the most overlooked options in the system. If you were married long enough, you may be able to claim a check based on your former spouse's work record, even though you're no longer together.

Claiming Benefits Based on an Ex-Spouse's Record

Just as a current spouse can claim on a partner's record, a former spouse may be able to do the same after a divorce.

This works a lot like the spousal benefit we covered earlier. If your former spouse earned quite a bit more than you over the years, the check available on their record may be larger than the one based on your own earnings. You compare the two and take the higher amount.

Say your own benefit is about $900 a month, and half of your former spouse's full amount works out to roughly $1,300. Just as for an active marriage, Social Security pays you the larger one, lifting your monthly check from $900 to about $1,300. You're not actually taking money from an ex-spouse; in fact, they're usually never even notified about it (more on this below). You're simply claiming the higher of two benefits you qualify for under Social Security. It's rightfully yours.

It feels backward, which is why so few people investigate it. Most assume that when a marriage ends, every financial connection ends with it. They can't imagine that a relationship from decades ago could still put money in their pocket today, and that assumption leaves a lot of legitimate benefits untouched.

The 10-Year Marriage Rule That Determines Eligibility

Your marriage generally must have lasted at least 10 years for you to claim on a former spouse's record.

That 10-year mark is the entry ticket, so to speak. Hit that point, and the door to these benefits can stay open after the divorce. Miss it by even a few months, and that door closes altogether.

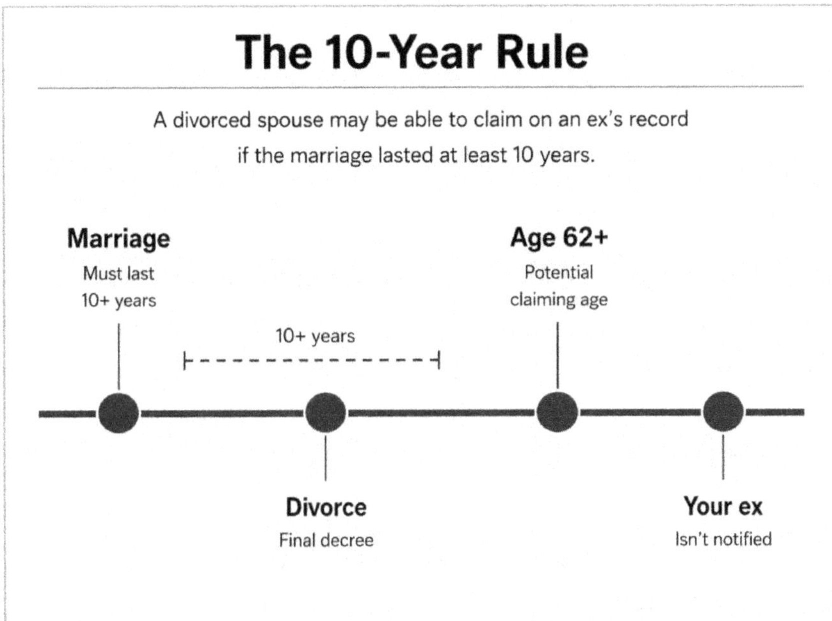

A marriage that lasted nine and a half years and one that lasted ten years and a day can lead to very different outcomes. If you were married anywhere near that line, confirm your exact marriage and divorce dates before you assume anything.

Can Remarriage Affect Your Eligibility?

This is where things get a little more nuanced. If you remarry, you can't collect benefits on a former spouse's record while that new marriage is in place.

But the details *can* work in your favor. If that later marriage ends, whether through divorce or the death of that spouse, your eligibility on the earlier former spouse's record can come back into play. The option isn't always gone for good. Usually, it just pauses while you're remarried.

Many get mixed up here, assuming that remarrying at any point permanently erases every prior option, or that staying single does the same. Neither is true. What matters when you claim is your *current* marital status, not every turn that got you there.

So if your marriage lasted at least ten years and you're not currently remarried, a benefit you never knew about may be waiting for you. Don't let an old assumption keep you from money that you have every right to claim. Check your dates and compare your options.

Can You Claim an Ex-Spouse's Benefit Without Affecting Them?

If you're afraid that claiming on a former spouse's record will reopen old conflict or take something from someone you'd rather not contact, the reality is far less dramatic.

Will Your Ex-Spouse Know You're Claiming Benefits?

No. Your former spouse isn't notified when you claim a benefit on their record. There's no letter or phone call, so put any fears of unwanted, awkward conversations to rest. This stays between you and Social Security.

Does Claiming on an Ex-Spouse's Record Reduce Their Benefit?

To answer the question that holds even generous people back, claiming on a former spouse's record doesn't reduce their benefit by a single dollar.

Their check stays exactly the same, and so does the check of any current spouse they may have. Social Security calculates your benefit on their record separately, without taking anything from them or anyone else tied to that record.

An easy way to think about it is that your claim runs *alongside* theirs, not out of it.

Rather than taking something from a former spouse, you're in fact claiming an amount that exists separately from that person's check. And there's no reason to feel guilty about that.

What Social Security Uses to Verify Eligibility

To approve your claim, Social Security needs to confirm a few basic facts. Mostly, it needs proof that the marriage happened and that it lasted long enough.

Gather these records before you apply so that the process goes more smoothly:

- Your marriage certificate, showing the date you were married
- Your divorce decree, showing the date the marriage legally ended
- Your former spouse's name (and Social Security number if you have it, though Social Security can often locate the record themselves)

The verification itself is routine. Social Security checks the dates, confirms the marriage reached the 10-year mark, and reviews your current marital status.

Pull out those two documents, your marriage certificate and divorce decree, and you remove most of the friction before you even sit down to apply.

What Happens If Your Ex-Spouse Passes Away

When a former spouse dies, your benefit options can shift in your favor, and the years you shared can keep protecting you long after the marriage ended.

Why an Ex-Spouse's Death Can Change Your Benefit Options

While your former spouse is alive, the benefit you can claim on their record is the divorced-spouse benefit, worth up to half of their full amount. After they die, a different and often larger option may apply.

As a surviving divorced spouse, you may qualify for a survivor benefit, which can be worth quite a bit more than the divorced-spouse benefit. The jump can be significant, sometimes moving from roughly half of their amount to something closer to the full amount. We'll go into the detailed survivor rules in the next chapter.

How Survivor Benefits Work for Divorced Spouses

Reach that 10-year mark mentioned earlier, and the protection can follow you long after the divorce. The rule applies twice, first to divorced-spouse benefits and then later to survivor benefits if your ex-spouse dies.

The reason so few people claim it is the same reason they miss the original benefit. After a divorce, most never revisit Social Security at all. They assume the matter became irrelevant years ago, and so they never check what a former spouse's death might mean for them.

3 Common Divorced-Survivor Scenarios

A small change in the facts can change the outcome. These examples below illustrate how the rules work in some of the situations you're most likely to encounter.

Scenario 1: Your former spouse dies before you file. *In that case, you may be able to claim a survivor benefit based on their record instead of the smaller divorced-spouse benefit. It's worth checking which option gives you the larger check.*

Scenario 2: Your former spouse dies after you've already claimed. *Here, you may be able to step up from the divorced-spouse benefit you were receiving to the larger survivor benefit. That earlier, smaller check isn't necessarily the end of the story.*

Scenario 3: You have your own benefit plus survivor options. *If your own earnings record produces a solid check, you compare it with the survivor benefit and take the higher of the two. You're not forced into the smaller option when a better one is available.*

When Major Life Changes Affect Your Benefits

If you carry one thing out of this chapter, make it this: Recheck your Social Security options whenever your life changes in a major way.

Several moments deserve a fresh look, such as:

- A divorce, especially one that crossed the 10-year mark
- A remarriage, which can pause or change your options
- The death of a former spouse, which can open a larger survivor benefit
- Your own retirement, when you finally compare every check available to you

Treat those life events as your cue to pull out the records and ask yourself, *Is there a better check available to me now than the one I assumed I was stuck with?* Quite often, the answer is yes.

CHAPTER 7:

HOW SURVIVOR BENEFITS WORK AFTER LOSING A CURRENT SPOUSE

Losing a spouse is one of the hardest things a person goes through, and in the middle of the grief, Social Security lands on your desk at the worst possible moment. The decisions feel urgent and the rules are unfamiliar. What's more, everyone seems to want an answer now. But one of the most expensive mistakes a widow or widower can make is filing too fast. A calm choice here can mean multiple thousands over the years ahead, so it's crucial to know the facts.

The most important thing to know up front is that you generally have more options than you realize, and you rarely have to rush.

Common Mistakes with Survivor Benefits

When a spouse dies, the survivor often files for the first benefit someone mentions, never realizing that a smarter order existed, but that mistake can shrink their income for years.

The Filing Mistake That Can Reduce Lifetime Survivor Income

Grief pushes people to act fast, and that's exactly when money slips away. The wrong filing order is hard to undo, and it can cost a survivor for the rest of their life.

> *Margaret lost her husband at 66, and the weeks that followed were a blur of phone calls and forms. When she sat down with Social Security, a representative explained that she could receive a survivor benefit based on her husband's record. It was larger than her own check, so she almost filed for it on the spot. Then she paused.*
>
> *She remembered that a friend had mentioned something about claiming order, so she decided to learn how it worked before signing anything. This was a smart move on Margaret's part.*
>
> *Margaret had two separate benefits she could draw from: her own retirement benefit and the survivor benefit on her husband's record. Those two benefits follow different rules and grow in different ways. Once she understood that, she found a sequence that left her with far more lifetime income than she would've received if she'd filed for the bigger check right away.*

Your Survivor Benefit or Your Retirement Benefit: Which Comes First?

This is the question at the center of the whole chapter. As a widow or widower, you may have access to two checks: your own retirement benefit and a survivor benefit based on your late spouse's record. You generally can't collect both at the same time, so the order matters.

Because these two benefits grow differently, you can sometimes start with one, let the other keep growing, and switch later to the larger amount. That sequence makes all the difference.

Don't assume that you must pick one benefit forever on day one. Pause, learn how each check works, and choose the order that gives you the most over your lifetime.

The Survivor Benefit Rules Every Widow & Widower Should Know

Before you can choose a smart sequence, you need a clear picture of how survivor benefits work. The rules are more flexible than you'd expect, and once you understand them, a lot of the mystery disappears.

Who Qualifies for Survivor Benefits?

If you were married to someone who earned Social Security, you may qualify for a survivor benefit when that person dies. In most cases, the marriage must have lasted at least nine months before death (this is different from the 10-year rule that applies to divorced spouses seeking benefits on an ex-spouse's record, including divorced-survivor benefits). However, there are exceptions in situations such as an accident.

Age is the next piece. You can generally claim a survivor benefit as early as age 60, which is earlier than your own retirement benefit allows. If you have a qualifying disability, that age can drop to 50. If you're caring for the deceased's young or disabled child, you may qualify at any age.

One of the most common misconceptions is that survivor benefits only go to people who never worked, but this is incorrect. Even if you had a full career and your own benefit, you may still qualify for a survivor benefit and choose whichever path serves you best.

When a Survivor Can Receive a Higher Monthly Benefit

As a couple, you were drawing two checks. After one of you dies, only one continues; the household doesn't keep both.

The upshot to this is that you keep the larger of the two. If your late spouse's benefit was bigger than yours, the survivor benefit raises your income to that higher amount. If your own check was larger, that's the one you keep. That's why the higher earner's claiming decision, which we covered in earlier chapters, matters so much for the spouse left behind.

How Filing Age Can Affect Survivor Benefit Amounts

Just like your own retirement benefit, the timing of a survivor claim affects the size of the check. Claim a survivor benefit before your Full Retirement Age, and the amount is reduced. Wait until your FRA, and you can receive the full survivor benefit, up to 100% of what your late spouse was receiving or was entitled to receive.

A survivor benefit doesn't grow past your FRA. Unlike your own retirement check, which keeps climbing until 70, it tops out at FRA, so there's no reason to delay it beyond that point.

It can be claimed as early as 60 in a reduced form, reaches its full amount at your FRA, and grows no further after that. Those three facts set up the filing tactics we turn to next.

The Claiming Strategies That Can Increase Lifetime Income

Because your own retirement benefit and a survivor benefit follow different timelines, you can often use them in a sequence that puts far more money in your pocket over the years.

The Claim-Now, Switch-Later Strategy

You can claim one benefit now and switch to the other later, choosing the order that lets the larger check grow as long as possible before you turn it on.

This works because survivor benefits and retirement benefits are separate checks with separate rules. Your own retirement benefit keeps growing if you delay it, all the way to age 70, through the delayed retirement credits we mentioned previously. A survivor benefit, by contrast, tops out at your Full Retirement Age and grows no further.

It's like having two savings accounts that grow at different speeds. You draw from the slower one first while the faster one keeps building, then switch once the faster one has grown as large as it ever will. The crucial part is knowing which check is which in your situation.

When Claiming Survivor Benefits Should Come First

In many cases, the smart move is to take the survivor benefit first and let your own retirement benefit grow. This tends to fit people whose own benefit will eventually be the larger of the two.

The survivor benefit maxes out at your FRA and stops growing, while your own retirement benefit keeps climbing until 70. So if your own check can grow past the survivor amount, you collect the survivor benefit now and let your own check grow in the background.

Then around age 70, you switch to your own retirement benefit once it's reached its peak. You spend years collecting survivor checks and still end up with the largest possible retirement check for the rest of your life.

So let's say that your survivor benefit is about $2,000 a month, while your own benefit would grow to roughly $2,600 by age 70. Taking the survivor benefit first lets you bring in income now, and then switching to your own check at 70 locks in the larger amount from that point forward. That sequence can mean a noticeably bigger check later when you may need it most.

When Claiming Your Own Retirement Benefit Should Come First

The opposite sequence can be just as smart, depending on your numbers.

This fits people whose survivor benefit will be the larger of the two. Remember, the survivor benefit reaches its full amount at

your Full Retirement Age. So if that survivor check is going to be bigger, you let it rise to that maximum while you collect your own smaller retirement benefit in the meantime.

> *Kate's own benefit is modest, perhaps around $1,100 a month, while her survivor benefit would reach about $2,300 at her Full Retirement Age. She can claim her own reduced benefit as early as 62 to bring in some income, then switch to the full survivor benefit once she reaches FRA. She collects checks the whole time and still steps up to the larger survivor amount later.*

How to Compare Your Options

First, determine the size of your own retirement benefit at your FRA and at 70, then find out the size of the survivor benefit at your FRA. Compare which one will be larger.

Once you know which check wins in the end, the strategy almost chooses itself. Claim the smaller one first, let the larger one grow to its peak, and switch when the time comes. That comparison is the heart of survivor planning, and it's well worth the phone call to confirm your exact numbers before you file.

4 Survivor-Benefit Scenarios That Produce Different Outcomes

Numbers make more sense when illustrated with real-life examples. These four widows face the same kind of decision, but each arrives at a different answer that fits her situation.

The Widow at Age 60

Jessica is 60 and recently widowed. Money is tight, and she needs income to keep things steady. She qualifies for a survivor benefit now, even though her own retirement benefit is still years away.

It's quite the trade-off. Claiming the survivor benefit at 60 means taking a reduced amount, since she's well before her Full Retirement Age. But if she needs the income to get by, that early survivor check can be the right call. She may also have the option to switch to her own retirement benefit later if it grows larger by 70.

The Widow at Age 67

Patricia is 67, at her Full Retirement Age, and weighing her own benefit against the survivor benefit. Her own check would be about $1,900, while the survivor benefit is around $2,100.

Because she's at her FRA, the survivor benefit is at its maximum and won't grow any further, but her own benefit could still climb until 70. So she might take the survivor benefit now and let her own check grow, then compare the two at 70 to see which one should be her benefit for life.

A Widow with a Small Retirement Benefit

Julia worked for only a few years and has a small retirement benefit of her own, maybe $600 a month. Her late husband earned far more, so the survivor benefit is clearly the bigger check.

For Julia, the survivor benefit will almost certainly drive the decision. She might claim her own small benefit early for some income, then step up to the full survivor benefit at her FRA. The survivor check is where her real protection lies.

A Widow with a Larger Retirement Benefit

Barbara had a long, well-paid career, and her own benefit will grow to about $2,800 by age 70. Her survivor benefit is around $2,200.

For Barbara, the comparison flips because her own benefit will eventually be the larger one. So the smart sequence is often to take the survivor benefit first, collect it for several years, and switch to her own bigger check at 70. She gets income now and the largest possible benefit later.

Notice the pattern across all four women. Each one compared her own benefit with her survivor benefit, figured out which would be larger, and claimed the smaller one first while letting the bigger one grow. Comparing the two before you file gives you a much stronger basis for your decision, so take your time, run your numbers, and find the sequence that fits your situation.

CHAPTER 8:

WORKING WHILE COLLECTING (& WHAT IT DOES TO YOUR CHECK)

Plenty of people picture retirement as a hard stop. One day you're working and the next you're not, then the checks simply start arriving. But real life is rarely that tidy. Many people claim Social Security and keep working, whether for the income, for a sense of purpose, or simply because they enjoy it. And while that's perfectly acceptable, it does come with a rule that's worth understanding before you file.

Working While Receiving Social Security

If you claim Social Security before your FRA and keep working, some of your benefits may be temporarily held back. The rule behind this is called the earnings test, and it trips up more retirees than almost anything else in the system. The Social Security Administration sets and updates the rules for this test each year.

The Rule That Can Reduce Your Social Security Checks While Working

The most important thing to know is that this rule changes at your Full Retirement Age. Before you reach that age, the earnings test applies, but once you hit it, the test disappears entirely. From that point on, you can earn any amount you want and your check won't be reduced at all.

This earnings test is kind of like a temporary speed bump on a road you're only driving for a few years. It slows things down for a stretch, then vanishes the moment you reach FRA. But just knowing that the bump is temporary changes how you feel about the whole trip.

Understanding the Earnings Test Before You File

So who does this apply to? The earnings test affects people who claim benefits before their Full Retirement Age and continue to earn money from work. If you wait until your FRA to claim, the test never touches you.

This applies to singles and couples alike, and each person is measured on their own earnings. If you're married and both of you claimed early, the test looks at each of your work incomes separately. Your spouse's paycheck doesn't count against your check, and yours doesn't count against theirs.

The biggest misunderstanding is the belief that working while collecting means that you lose those benefits for good, but that's not how it works (and we'll get to those reassuring details in a moment). For now, just be aware that the earnings test is temporary and that the money it holds back isn't gone.

Which Income Can Reduce Your Social Security Benefits?

Not every kind of income counts toward the earnings test. The rule only looks at money you earn from working.

Earned income means either wages from a job (the paycheck you bring home) or net profit from self-employment (the income from running your own business). Those dollars are what the earnings test measures.

A great deal of retirement income doesn't count at all. The following sources generally don't trigger the earnings test whatsoever:

- Withdrawals from retirement accounts like a 401(k) or IRA
- Pension payments
- Investment income such as interest, dividends, and capital gains
- Rental income from property you own

This means that you could pull a healthy sum from your IRA in a given year, and that money wouldn't reduce your Social Security check one bit. Only the income from actually working counts.

What Counts Toward the $24,480 Limit

For the earnings test, only earned income counts.

Counts	Does NOT count
Wages	Pensions
Self-employment income	IRA withdrawals
Bonuses	Investment income
Commissions	Annuities

So if you plan to work while claiming early, focus on your wages and self-employment profit, because those are the only dollars the earnings test is concerned with.

Why a Reduced Check Doesn't Always Mean Lost Benefits

This is the part of the chapter that'll likely put you at ease more than any other. The benefits held back by the earnings test are set aside and returned to you later in the form of a larger check. We'll see below exactly how that works.

How Much Can the Earnings Test Reduce Your Benefits?

The earnings test works off a yearly income limit that the Social Security Administration adjusts each year. Earn below that limit, and nothing is held back, but if you earn above it, and Social Security holds back a portion of your check based on how far over the limit you went. This extra amount above the limit is often called your excess earnings.

In the years before Full Retirement Age, the rule generally holds back one dollar of benefits for every two dollars you earn above the limit. A simple, rounded example makes that clear:

> *Tom claimed early and works part-time. The yearly limit is $24,480, and Tom earns about $30,480. That puts him $6,000 over the limit. Because the rule holds back one dollar for every two dollars over, Social Security would hold back about $3,000 of his benefits for that year.*

The earnings test is less restrictive during the year you reach Full Retirement Age. In that specific year, the limit is much higher and the formula holds back only one dollar for every *three* you earn above it, right up until the month you hit your FRA. After that month, the test stops completely.

Why Withheld Benefits Aren't Gone Forever

As mentioned above, Social Security keeps track of the money held back by the earnings test and gives it back to you once you reach your FRA. The way it does this is through a recalculation.

When you reach your FRA, Social Security looks at how many months of benefits it held back and adjusts your monthly check upward to make up for them. Your check goes up and stays up for the rest of your life.

In this regard, it's less like a tax and more like a savings account you didn't know you had. The money you couldn't collect while working gets credited back to you in the form of bigger checks later, paid out over the years ahead.

How Withheld Benefits Are Recalculated

Let's follow Tom a little further so you can see the whole arc.

> *During his early years of claiming, the earnings test held back some of his benefits because he kept working. He felt those smaller checks at the time, and it was frustrating.*
>
> *Then Tom reached his FRA. Social Security counted up the months of benefits it had held back over the years and recalculated his monthly amount. His check stepped up to a higher level to account for everything that had been set aside.*
>
> *From that point forward, Tom collects a larger check for the rest of his life. He didn't lose those early benefits at all. He simply received them later, spread across a bigger monthly payment.*

Just remember: If the earnings test holds back part of your check, you're not giving that money away. You get credit for it at Full Retirement Age. So work if you want or need to, knowing that the system will square up with you later.

Planning Work & Social Security Together

Now let's turn this into a plan, because when done thoughtfully, continued work can actually raise your future check while keeping your income steady today.

How Working Longer Can Increase Future Benefits

You'll recall that your benefit is built from your highest 35 years of earnings. Every year you keep working gives you a chance to replace a weak early year, or one of those empty zero years, with a stronger one, a swap that can nudge your benefit upward.

This is the same idea we covered earlier, the 35-year recalculation working in your favor. Each new year of solid earnings is a chance to rewrite your benefit formula with a better number, and the added bonus is that it's also income in the meantime.

> *Rachel had a couple of low-earning years early in her career. By working two more years at a good salary in her 60s, those strong years replace the weak ones in her record. Her monthly benefit climbs as a result, and that bump lasts for the rest of Rachel's life.*

Avoiding Surprise Reductions in Your Monthly Check

If you do plan to claim early and keep working, a little timing awareness goes a long way. The goal is to avoid being caught off guard when a check comes in smaller than you expected.

The simple move is to estimate your work income for the year and compare it against the earnings limit before you file. If you know that you'll earn well above the limit, you can expect some benefits to be held back and plan your budget around it, with no surprises and no scramble.

For some people, this comparison leads to a cleaner choice. If you're going to keep working full-time at a strong salary anyway, it can make more sense to delay claiming until your Full Retirement Age, when the earnings test no longer applies and your check is larger.

Working Longer, Claiming Smarter

The smartest approach is to line up your work plans and your claiming decision so that they support each other. They're two pieces of the same picture rather than separate choices.

> *Jay plans to work part-time until 67 and then fully retire. Because his earnings are modest and he reaches his FRA soon, claiming early may cost him little to nothing in held-back benefits, and his continued work may even raise his future check.*
>
> *But then there's Darryl, who plans to keep earning a full salary into his late 60s. For him, waiting to claim often makes more sense, since filing early would trigger the earnings test and lock in a smaller check at the same time.*

The practical step is to look at your work plans and your claiming age together, then choose the combination that fits your life.

PART II

WRAP-UP

You've now worked through the second question in the Money Code Framework: *How do I maximize household benefits?* Let's gather the key points before moving on.

The Core Ideas

Married couples do better when they coordinate their claiming decisions instead of filing separately. Spousal, divorced-spouse, and survivor benefits can add a great deal of money to your household, and they're easy to overlook. Also, work income can change the timing of when you claim (though it rarely costs you benefits for good).

Common Household Benefit Mistakes

Watch for the traps that catch people most often:

- Spouses claiming without a shared household strategy
- Missing survivor or divorced-spouse benefits you qualify for
- Overlooking how work income affects the timing of your claim

Your Part II Action Plan

Steps to take before you continue with this book:

1. Compare all the benefit options available to you and your household
2. Identify the higher earner, and understand how that decision shapes household income
3. Determine whether spousal, survivor, or divorced-spouse benefits may apply
4. Estimate whether work income could affect your benefits before Full Retirement Age

With your household benefits in view, the next piece is protecting what you keep. Part III turns us toward taxes and the surprising bite they can take, starting with why the tax man takes a cut of your benefits in the first place.

PART III:

PROTECT WHAT YOU'VE EARNED

Collecting your benefits is one thing, but *keeping* them is another thing entirely. Taxes and withdrawal decisions work in the background to determine how much of each check you actually get to spend, and a little planning in this area can save you thousands over the course of your retirement.

CHAPTER 9:

THE TAX TRAP HIDDEN INSIDE SOCIAL SECURITY

The idea that the government might tax the very benefits it sends you feels almost backward, but for many retirees, that's exactly what happens, and it tends to hit at the worst possible moment.

Once you understand why benefits get taxed and what triggers that tax, you can plan around it.

The Tax Surprise for Retirees

Plenty of people reach retirement assuming that their Social Security check arrives completely tax-free, and that assumption feels reasonable. You already paid taxes during your working years, so why would the government tax this money, too? But retirement introduces a new set of tax rules, and Social Security is part of them.

What Triggers Taxes on Social Security

It's an easy rule to overlook, because nothing about your monthly check hints that taxes may be waiting later. The surprise often arrives when it's time to file your tax return.

> *Howard learned this lesson the hard way. He retired at 66, proud of the nest egg he'd built. Between his Social Security check and steady withdrawals from his retirement accounts, he felt comfortable. He assumed his Social Security income was his to keep.*
>
> *Then his first tax season as a retiree rolled around. His accountant explained that a large portion of his Social Security benefits were taxable because his account withdrawals had pushed his total income high enough to trigger it. Howard was stunned; he'd never heard that his benefits could be taxed at all.*

That feeling of being blindsided by a rule no one bothered to mention is exactly what we want to spare you.

Whether your benefits get taxed depends on the benefits themselves, but also on your total income from *all* sources. The more income you bring in from other areas, the more of your Social Security check can become taxable.

A Bigger Check Doesn't Always Mean More Money in Your Pocket

A larger Social Security check is obviously a good thing, but the number on the check isn't always the number you keep. It's what lands in your pocket after taxes that matters.

Think of this like a paycheck during your working years. Your salary may have been one number, but your take-home pay was smaller after taxes came out, right? Retirement income can work the same way, because gross and net aren't the same thing.

That distinction matters when you plan. If you focus only on the size of your check and ignore the tax side of things, you can end up surprised by how much less you really have to spend. The goal is to protect your net income, the money you can actually *use*.

The Income Formula That Determines Whether Your Benefits Are Taxable

So how does the government decide whether your benefits get taxed? It uses a measure called combined income, sometimes called provisional income. To calculate combined income, take your regular taxable income, add any tax-free interest you earned, then add half of your Social Security benefits. It's like filling a measuring cup; your other income makes up most of what goes in, then half of your Social Security gets poured on top. The higher that cup fills, the more of your benefits may become taxable. Notice what that means in real life. Half of your benefit is always part of the recipe, but *only* half. Your other income does most of the work.

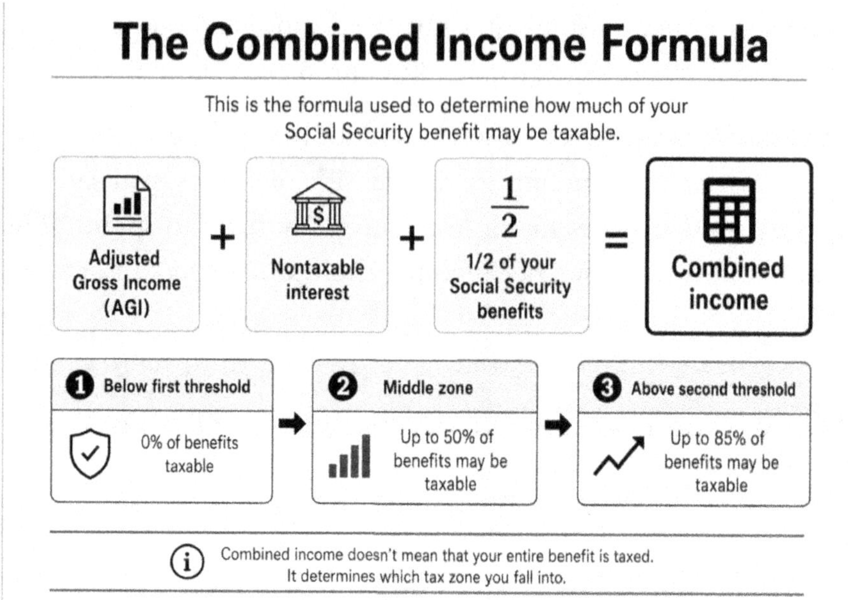

The Income Thresholds That Trigger Social Security Taxes

Now let's get specific about where those lines fall. As illustrated in the graphs, the system uses a set of income thresholds to decide how much of your benefit becomes taxable. Once you see how the tiers work, the whole thing stops feeling random.

The 50% & 85% Thresholds Explained

Social Security Tax Threshold Map

These combined-income thresholds determine how much of your benefit may be taxable.

	0% taxable zone	Up to 50% taxable zone	Up to 85% taxable zone
Single filer	Below $25,000	$25,000–$34,000	Above $34,000
Married filing jointly	Below $32,000	$32,000–$44,000	Above $44,000

These are combined-income thresholds under current law, and they're not indexed for inflation.

Combined income = AGI + nontaxable interest + 1/2 of Social Security benefits.

There are three possible outcomes for your benefits, and they depend on where your combined income lands. Think of them as three tiers stacked one above the next.

- **None of your benefit is taxed:** If your combined income stays low, your Social Security check is left completely untouched
- **Up to half of your benefit is taxed:** Cross the first line, and as much as 50% of your benefit can become taxable
- **Up to 85% of your benefit is taxed:** Cross the second and higher line, and as much as 85% of your benefit can become taxable

But here's a little bit of relief: Even in the worst case, no more than 85% of your benefit is ever taxable. At least 15% always stays protected, no matter how high your income climbs.

It also helps to understand what those percentages mean. The 50% and 85% figures describe how much of your benefit can be taxed, not the tax rate itself. So you're simply counting up to 85% of your check as income on your tax return, not the entire thing.

When Benefits Become Taxable

Crossing one of these thresholds is usually the result of income arriving from more than one place, and these two examples below demonstrate clearly how it happens.

> *Ruth is a single retiree. Her Social Security benefit is modest, and she takes only small withdrawals from her savings. Her combined income stays below the first threshold, so none of her benefit is taxed. She keeps her full check.*
>
> *Donald is also single. He collects a similar Social Security benefit, but he also takes larger withdrawals from his retirement account and receives a small pension. Those extra dollars lift his combined income above the higher line. As a result, up to 85% of his benefit counts as taxable income.*

The difference between Ruth and Donald had nothing to do with their benefits, but rather everything else flowing into the measuring cup alongside them. They simply managed their other income differently.

More Retirees Are Paying Taxes on Social Security Than Ever Before

The income thresholds that decide all this have stayed roughly the same for decades. They just weren't designed to rise with inflation the way many other tax figures do. Meanwhile, incomes, savings balances, and the cost of living have all gone up.

Ordinary incomes have risen while the thresholds stayed put, so more and more people cross those lines. A level of income that once kept benefits tax-free can now tip a retiree into taxable territory.

You can't change the thresholds, but you *can* manage the income that flows toward them. Knowing that the lines exist is the first step in planning your income so that you stay on the side that works best for you.

Income Sources That Can Increase Your Social Security Tax Bill

Your benefits get taxed based on the other income you bring in, which raises the natural question: *Which sources move the needle most?*

Retirement Accounts That Push Benefits Into Taxable Territory

For most retirees, the biggest driver is withdrawals from traditional retirement accounts. Money you pull from a traditional IRA or a 401(k) counts as taxable income, and it goes straight into that combined-income measuring cup.

This is the piece that surprised Howard at the start of this chapter. Every dollar he withdrew from his accounts added to his combined income, which in turn made more of his Social Security benefit taxable. The withdrawals themselves were taxed, and they also pulled his benefits into taxable territory.

If a retiree decides to take a large withdrawal one year to cover a home repair, that one big withdrawal can lift his combined income high enough to tax a much larger share of his benefits for that year.

Tax Triggers: Pensions, Investment & Part-Time Work

Retirement account withdrawals are the most common culprit, but several other income sources count toward your combined income, too.

- **Pension income:** A monthly pension is taxable income, and it adds to your combined income like any other dollar
- **Investment income:** Interest, dividends, and capital gains from your accounts all count. Even tax-free interest gets added back in for this calculation
- **Part-time work:** Wages from a job in retirement count toward your combined income as well, separate from the earnings test we covered earlier

Notice how these add up? A pension here, some dividends there, a bit of part-time work, and your combined income rises piece by piece. Together, those sources can push you across one of those thresholds, but at least they're predictable. That means you can total them up ahead of time and plan around them.

The Coordination Mistake That Gets the Tax Man Knocking

When you look at all your income as one connected picture, you can adjust the timing and the amounts to keep your combined income where you want it. A little coordination can mean a noticeably smaller tax bill.

But not every dollar of retirement income lands in the measuring cup. Money you draw from a Roth account, for example, generally doesn't count toward your combined income. But it all comes down to timing, which matters just as much as the amount.

Taxes on your Social Security benefits depend on both the amount and timing of your other income. The next chapter turns that into action, with smart ways to draw from your accounts so that you keep more of each payment.

CHAPTER 10:

KEEPING MORE OF YOUR CHECK WITH SMART WITHDRAWALS

The income thresholds are one piece of the puzzle, but how and when you draw from your accounts is the piece you can control. Used well, your withdrawal order and timing can save you more money than you were expecting over the course of your retirement. All you need are a few simple ideas about how different accounts are taxed and, how to draw from them in a smart sequence.

The Withdrawal Order That Can Save Thousands in Taxes

Most people retire with money spread across a few types of accounts, then pull from whatever feels easiest, never noticing that the order alone can change the tax bill. The withdrawal order you settle into during your first few years of retirement can shape your tax bill for years to come.

Not All Retirement Dollars Are Taxed the Same

The dollars in your retirement accounts aren't all treated the same by the IRS. They fall into three buckets, and each one plays by its own rules.

> **Taxable accounts:** *These are your regular savings and brokerage accounts. You already paid tax on the money you put in, so only the growth and earnings are taxed, often at lower rates. Because you've already settled up with the IRS on the principal, pulling from these accounts tends to add very little to your taxable income. That's exactly why they make such a gentle starting point.*
>
> **Tax-deferred accounts:** *These are your traditional IRA and 401(k). You didn't pay tax on this money when it went in, so every dollar you pull out later counts as taxable income.*
>
> **Roth accounts:** *These are your Roth IRA and Roth 401(k). You already paid tax on this money, so qualified withdrawals come out completely tax-free. That tax-free status is rare and valuable, which is why so many retirees treat these accounts as the bucket they save for last.*

Those three buckets are like different faucets. One drips a little tax, one runs full tax, and one runs clean.

The Withdrawal Order That Changes What You Keep

A solid starting point for many retirees is to draw from taxable accounts first, tax-deferred next, and Roth last.

Why that order? Because spending taxable savings first often keeps your taxable income lower in your early retirement years. That gives your tax-deferred money more time to grow, and it lets your Roth money (the tax-free bucket) sit untouched for as long as possible.

> *Elle needs about $40,000 a year on top of Social Security. Early in retirement, she pulls that money from her regular savings account. Because those withdrawals barely count as taxable income, her combined income stays low, and very little of her Social Security check gets taxed. She keeps more of each dollar simply by choosing the right faucet first.*

Now compare that with a retiree who pulls the same $40,000 straight from a traditional IRA. Every one of those dollars counts as taxable income. That raises the combined income we covered in the last chapter, which then causes more of the Social Security check to be taxed.

Matching Withdrawals to Your Own Situation

That order is a sensible default rather than a rule carved in stone. The best sequence depends on your mix of accounts and your income needs.

Some people do better by blending the buckets. You might pull most of your income from taxable savings while taking a small amount from your traditional IRA each year, just enough to use up the lower tax brackets without crossing a threshold. That kind of mixing can keep combined income steadier and taxes on your benefits lower.

> *Carl and Diane are a married couple who need about $50,000 a year beyond Social Security. Rather than draining one account, they take $35,000 from taxable savings and a steady $15,000 from the traditional IRA each year. The smaller IRA piece fits neatly*

inside the lower brackets, keeps their combined income steady, and slowly trims the balance that their future required withdrawals will be based on. It's the same income but with a smoother tax path.

The most common mistake here is autopilot. People drain one account because it feels simplest, and meanwhile they never notice the tax cost piling up beside it. Just a few minutes of planning each year can prevent that.

A smarter sequence generally looks like this:

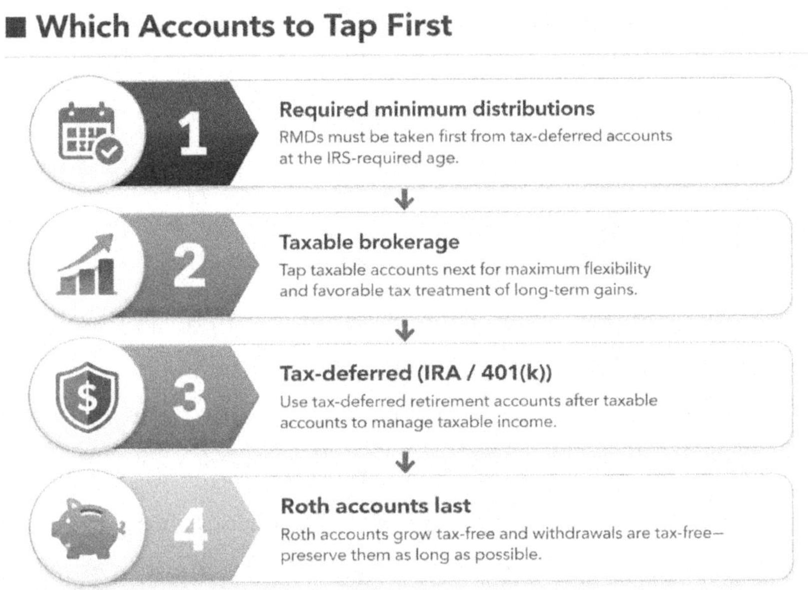

The key is to be aware of which of your three buckets you're drawing from, lean toward taxable first and Roth last as a starting point, and adjust based on your numbers. Follow that advice, and you'll be able to protect a meaningful piece of your Social Security check year after year.

The Hidden Connection Between Withdrawals & Social Security Taxes

You already know that other income determines how much of your Social Security check gets taxed. Withdrawals are a big part of that other income, which means that the choices you make about pulling money are tied directly to your benefit taxes. Let's connect those dots clearly below.

The Withdrawal Mistake That Pushes You Into a Higher Tax Zone

Remember the combined-income measuring cup? Every dollar you pull from a traditional IRA or 401(k) goes straight into that cup. The more you withdraw in a year, the higher the cup fills, and the more of your benefit can become taxable.

So if you reach for the tax-deferred bucket first, you're adding fully taxable dollars to the cup right away, often pushing yourself across a threshold sooner than necessary. Drawing from taxable savings or Roth money instead keeps that cup lower.

This comes down to what each withdrawal does to the taxability of your Social Security check sitting right beside it; it's not just about the withdrawal itself. The two move together.

Tax Consequences of Large Withdrawals

Big, one-time withdrawals are where people get caught. If you decide to pull a large sum from your traditional IRA in one year to remodel a kitchen or help a grandchild with college, it can hit you two ways at once. That withdrawal gets taxed as income on its own *and* it can lift your combined income high enough to tax a much larger share of your Social Security benefit for that year. One decision, but two tax hits.

> *Dennis pulls $50,000 from a traditional IRA in one year for a home project. In a normal year, only a small share of his benefit is taxable. In the big-withdrawal year, the extra income pushes him into the top tier, and suddenly up to 85% of his benefit counts as taxable income. The kitchen cost more than the contractor's bill.*

Withdrawal Decisions Affect More Than This Year's Tax Bill

But a withdrawal decision is rarely just a one-year event; it can ripple through several years of taxes and several years of benefit taxation.

That same $50,000 kitchen project, for example, might've been spread across two or three years instead of one. Smaller withdrawals each year could've kept combined income lower, protected more of the Social Security check, and reduced the total tax paid over that stretch.

So think beyond a single calendar year when you plan a withdrawal. Ask not only what it costs in taxes this year, but also what it does to your benefit taxes this year and next. We'll pull all this together into one full retirement-income picture later in the guide.

Tax Planning Decisions That Affect Retirement Income

A few specific moves make a substantial difference in what you keep. You just need to know they exist and think a year or two ahead. Below, we'll take a look at the ones that matter most.

When Roth Conversations Make Sense

A Roth conversion is simpler than it sounds. You move money from your traditional IRA into a Roth IRA, pay the tax on that amount now, and in exchange, that money grows tax-free and comes out tax-free later.

Why would you choose to pay tax sooner? Timing. There's often a window in early retirement, after you stop working but before larger income sources kick in, when your taxable income drops. Converting some money during those lower-income years can mean paying tax at a relatively low rate now instead of a steeper rate later.

The payoff shows up down the road. Money in a Roth account doesn't count toward the combined income that taxes your Social Security check, and Roth IRAs aren't subject to the forced withdrawals we'll cover in a moment. So a few well-timed conversions can lighten your tax load for the rest of your life.

When a Roth Conversion Can Backfire

A Roth conversion is a tool, and just like any tool, it can be used at the wrong time. The most common misstep is converting too much in a single year.

The amount you convert counts as taxable income for that year. Convert a large sum all at once, and you can push yourself into a higher tax bracket, tax more of your Social Security benefit, and even raise certain Medicare costs (more on that in a bit).

The fix here is patience. Most people do better converting smaller amounts over several lower-income years, filling the lower brackets without spilling over. It's like moving a woodpile one armful at a time instead of hauling the whole stack at once. With conversions, timing and size are everything.

Understanding Required Minimum Distributions

Once you reach a certain age, the government requires you to pull money out of your traditional IRA and 401(k) whether you need it or not. These forced withdrawals are called Required Minimum Distributions, or RMDs.

The tricky thing about these is that they can sneak up on people. If you let a large traditional balance sit untouched for years, those required withdrawals can be sizable once they begin. Under current rules, they generally start at age 73. All that money counts as taxable income, which can cause more of your Social Security check to be taxed and push up your tax bill.

This is exactly why planning earlier matters. Drawing modest amounts from traditional accounts in your early retirement years, or converting some to a Roth, can shrink the balance those required withdrawals are based on later. A little action now can keep those required withdrawals from turning into a tax problem later.

You have years, not days, to chip away at a large traditional balance, so there's no need to feel pressured about this. The point is simply to start noticing it now while you still have plenty of low-tax ways to bring it down on your own terms.

Planning Taxes Across Multiple Years

The simple version goes like this. In lower-income years, you might draw a bit more from traditional accounts or convert some money to a Roth, deliberately using up the lower tax brackets. In higher-income years, you lean on taxable savings or Roth money to keep combined income down. You're smoothing income so that you don't get walloped in any one year.

You don't have to map out decades for this to help. Even looking just one or two years ahead, then asking which bucket to draw from next, can keep more of your Social Security check in your pocket.

Once a year before the calendar turns, spend a half hour estimating next year's income and deciding which bucket to lean on. That small check-in is often all it takes to spot a low-income window worth using, or a big withdrawal worth spreading out. Later in the guide, we'll bring claiming, taxes, withdrawals, and Medicare into one coordinated plan.

PART III

WRAP-UP

You have now worked through the third question in the Money Code Framework: how do I keep more of my money? Let's tighten up what you have learned before moving on.

The Core Ideas

Taxes can take a real bite out of retirement income, but none of it's random. The order in which you draw from your accounts affects how much you keep. And Social Security, taxes, and retirement accounts work together as one connected picture rather than separate pieces.

Common Tax Planning Mistakes

Keep an eye on these three traps:

- Ignoring the fact that your Social Security benefits can become taxable
- Making large withdrawals without a tax strategy behind them
- Waiting until required withdrawals create a tax problem you could've prevented

Your Part III Action Plan

Steps to take before you head to the next part of the book:

1. Estimate whether your Social Security benefits may become taxable
2. Create a preliminary withdrawal order for your retirement accounts
3. Identify any future Roth conversion or required-withdrawal planning opportunities
4. Flag any retirement-income decisions that could raise your taxes unnecessarily

With taxes handled, the final piece is the health aspect of all this. Part IV turns to Medicare, where a few timing decisions can either protect your monthly check or chip away at it, starting with how to handle Medicare without the headache.

PART IV:

MEDICARE & THE WHOLE PLAN

Healthcare is the piece that ties everything together, because Medicare costs come straight out of your Social Security check and climb with your income. These chapters show you how to dodge the lifelong enrollment traps, plan around the income surcharges, and pull claiming, taxes, and Medicare into one coordinated plan.

CHAPTER 11:

MEDICARE WITHOUT THE HEADACHE

Medicare is a health decision, but it's also one of the biggest money decisions of your retirement. This is because the premiums come straight out of your Social Security check, and a few choices you make around age 65 can raise those premiums for the rest of your life. Get them right and the rest is mostly paperwork. Otherwise, you'll pay for it every single month.

All you need is a handful of decisions and to remain aware of the deadlines tied to them.

The Medicare Mistakes That Can Follow You for Life

Some retirement choices give you a clean reset if you change your mind, but a few Medicare decisions don't. The moves you make around age 65 in terms of timing can lock in higher costs that stay with you as long as you have coverage, so they deserve a solid look before those deadlines show up.

Why Medicare Affects More Than Your Healthcare Costs

Once you're on Medicare and collecting Social Security, your Part B premium is usually taken straight out of your Social Security check before you ever see it. Your healthcare costs and your retirement income are tied tightly together.

This means that a higher Medicare premium shrinks your spendable income. The check you actually deposit is your benefit *minus* that premium. If you plan around the gross number alone, you'll be off by a good chunk of money every single month.

That's exactly why the topic of Medicare belongs in a Social Security guide. They're separate programs, but they meet inside your monthly check, and the decisions you make about one affect what you keep from the other.

The Age-65 Decision That Confuses Millions of Americans

Medicare eligibility generally begins at 65 no matter when you decide to start your Social Security check. You might wait until 70 to claim your benefit and still need to deal with Medicare at 65.

This trips people up all the time. They assume that the two start together, so they either claim Social Security early just to get Medicare, or they ignore Medicare because they're not ready to claim their benefit yet. Both mistakes can cost you.

Keep these two decisions in separate boxes. One is about when your retirement income starts, and the other is about when your health coverage starts. They can happen at different times, and they often should.

The Enrollment Deadlines You Don't Want to Miss

Medicare runs on deadlines, and missing one is where the long-lasting costs begin. There are three windows worth knowing.

- **Initial Enrollment Period:** This is your first window, a seven-month stretch around your 65th birthday. It covers the three months before your birthday month, the month itself, and the three months after.
- **Special Enrollment Period:** If you're still working at 65 and covered by an employer health plan, you may be able to delay Medicare and sign up later without penalty through this special window.
- **General Enrollment Period:** This is the catch-up window for people who missed their first chance and didn't qualify for a special one. It works, but it can come with penalties.

Your Initial Enrollment Period is like an on-ramp. Get on at the right time, and things usually move smoothly. Miss it without a valid reason, and you may wind up regretting it. But unlike a simple traffic decision, this mistake will stay with you for years.

The Penalties That Can Follow You for Life

Sign up late without a valid reason, and Medicare can add a permanent penalty to your premiums.

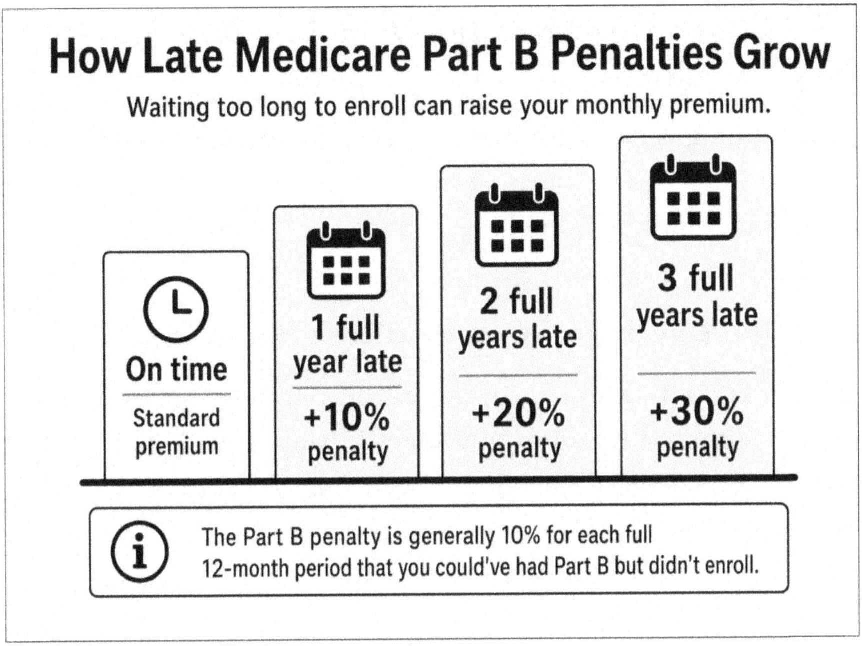

For each full year you could've enrolled in Part B but didn't, your monthly premium can rise by about 10%, and that increase generally lasts as long as you have Part B. Wait three years without coverage, and you could be looking at roughly 30% more every month.

The Part D penalty works in much the same way for prescription drug coverage. Go too long without creditable drug coverage, and a small permanent surcharge gets added to your Part D premium later.

Mark your enrollment window on the calendar now, figure out whether a special window applies to you, and don't let the date pass you by. A few minutes of attention today is lifelong protection for your check.

The Medicare Coverage Decisions Every New Retiree Faces

Once timing is handled, the next job is knowing what Medicare covers. It comes in parts, each with its own role. We've laid everything out for you below.

Hospital Coverage: What Medicare Part A Pays For

Part A is your hospital coverage, the part that steps in when you're admitted to a hospital, need a stay in a skilled nursing facility after a hospital visit, or use hospice care. It generally comes with no monthly premium because you already paid for it through years of payroll taxes during your working life.

But what Part A doesn't cover matters just as much. You can still face deductibles and other charges during a long stay, and it doesn't cover everyday medical care outside the hospital. That everyday care is where the next part comes in.

Medical Coverage: What Medicare Part B Pays For

Part B is your medical coverage, the part that handles ordinary healthcare. It covers doctor visits, outpatient care, preventive screenings, lab work, and a wide range of services you use without being admitted to a hospital.

Unlike Part A, Part B comes with a monthly premium. This is the premium that usually gets pulled from your Social Security check, which is exactly why it ties your healthcare costs to your retirement income.

Part B also comes with a yearly deductible, after which you usually pay a share of the cost for covered services. So it covers a lot of your routine care, but not everything automatically. Knowing that upfront helps you plan for the gaps instead of being surprised by them.

Comparing Medicare Coverage Options

Beyond the basic hospital and medical coverage, you'll run into two more letters that matter: Part C and Part D. These choices shape how the rest of your coverage fits together.

> **Part C, also called Medicare Advantage:** *An all-in-one alternative offered by private insurers. Instead of using the original parts separately, you get your coverage bundled into a single plan that often includes extra benefits.*
>
> **Part D, prescription drug coverage:** *Helps pay for your medications. Original Medicare doesn't include drug coverage on its own, so Part D takes care of that through a separate plan.*

With Original Medicare, you build coverage piece by piece and usually add a Part D plan for drugs. With Medicare Advantage, you trade that do-it-yourself setup for one bundled plan, usually with its own network of doctors. We'll compare the two paths more closely in a moment.

The Healthcare Costs Medicare Doesn't Fully Cover

Medicare covers a great deal, but some costs remain your responsibility, and planning for them helps keep your retirement budget on track. The big one is long-term care. If you ever need extended help with daily living, such as a long stay in a nursing home or ongoing in-home care, Medicare generally doesn't cover it, which can catch a lot of families at the worst possible moment.

Routine dental, vision, and hearing care are the other common gaps. Original Medicare usually doesn't pay for regular cleanings, eyeglasses, or hearing aids. Some Medicare Advantage plans do offer limited help with these, which is one reason people consider them.

So you need to know what Medicare covers *and* what it doesn't so that you can plan separately for dental, vision, hearing, and especially long-term care.

The Medicare Coverage Decisions That Shape Retirement Healthcare Costs

With the different parts sorted out, two bigger decisions still shape your costs: proving you had coverage while you delayed Medicare, and which path you choose to fill Medicare's gaps.

When Employer Coverage Lets You Delay Medicare

Remember those late-enrollment penalties from earlier? There's a way to delay Medicare without triggering them, and it hinges on one phrase worth knowing: creditable coverage.

This simply means health coverage that Medicare considers at least as good as its own. If you keep working past 65 and stay on a solid employer health plan, that plan will often count as creditable coverage. As long as you have it, you can delay Medicare and avoid the late penalties when you finally enroll.

That's how someone working into their late 60s stays protected. They keep their employer plan, skip Medicare for the time being, and use a Special Enrollment Period to sign up later without penalty once that job-based coverage ends. The system is built to allow exactly this (as long as the coverage qualifies).

But not every kind of coverage counts as creditable, and this is where a lot of people get burned. Retiree coverage and COBRA (the coverage you can continue after leaving a job) often don't qualify as creditable for delaying Medicare. Many assume that just any insurance will protect them, then find out the hard way that it didn't.

When you delay Medicare because of employer coverage, ask your plan for written proof that the coverage is creditable and keep it somewhere safe. If Medicare ever questions your timing, that letter is what spares you a lifelong penalty.

So if you plan to work past 65, confirm in writing that your employer plan counts as creditable coverage and keep that proof. If you're leaning on retiree coverage or COBRA, don't assume that it qualifies. Check before your enrollment window passes.

Medicare Advantage vs. Medigap: Two Very Different Paths

Once you're enrolled, you face one of the biggest coverage decisions in retirement. In most cases, you choose one of two paths to handle the costs Medicare leaves behind.

The first pairs Original Medicare with a Medigap policy. Medigap, also called Medicare Supplement insurance, is private coverage that fills in the deductibles and cost-sharing that

Original Medicare leaves to you. It smooths out the rough spots so that your out-of-pocket surprises get smaller.

The second path is Medicare Advantage, the all-in-one Part C plan we mentioned earlier. A private plan bundles your coverage together, often includes drug coverage, and may add extras like some dental or vision help. In exchange, you usually agree to use the plan's network of doctors and hospitals.

Let's compare the two paths in the ways that matter most to your wallet and your daily life.

> **Cost:** *Medigap plans usually carry a higher monthly premium, but they make your costs more predictable when you need care. Medicare Advantage plans often have lower monthly premiums, sometimes very low ones, but you usually pay as you go through copays when you actually use services. One trades a steadier premium for fewer surprises, while the other trades a lower premium for more variation.*
>
> **Provider flexibility:** *With Original Medicare and a Medigap plan, you can generally see any doctor or hospital in the country that accepts Medicare (which is most of them). With Medicare Advantage, you usually stay inside the plan's network, and going outside it can cost more (or may not be covered at all).*
>
> **Network considerations:** *This is where your daily life comes into play. If you travel often or split the year between two states, the broad access of Original Medicare with Medigap can be a real comfort. If you're happy with local doctors and like the idea of extra benefits rolled into one plan, Medicare Advantage may fit you just fine.*

So choose the path that matches how you actually live, as well as your healthcare needs. A low premium that doesn't cover your doctors is no bargain, and a higher premium that buys peace of mind can be money well spent.

Medicare, Medicaid & the Long-Term Care Confusion

Medicare is the health coverage you earned through work, available at 65 regardless of income. Medicaid is a separate program based on financial need that helps cover costs for people with limited income and assets. One is tied to your work history, and the other to your finances.

Medicaid enters the conversation because Medicare generally doesn't pay for long-term care, such as an extended nursing home stay. Medicaid often does, which is why many families end up considering it once long-term care becomes a very real and expensive need.

The common misconception is that Medicare will take care of a nursing home later on, but it generally won't. Knowing that now lets you plan for long-term care as its own separate issue instead of assuming that it's already handled.

Choosing Coverage That Fits Your Situation

Ask yourself how often you see doctors, whether you have specialists you want to keep, and how much you travel. Then ask what monthly premium feels manageable and how much surprise cost you can absorb. Your answers usually point pretty clearly toward one path or the other.

The two programs are easy to confuse, so it helps to set them side by side.

Medicare vs. Medicaid

These programs sound similar, but they serve different purposes.

Medicare	Medicaid
Age 65+ (mostly)	Income-based
Hospital & doctor	Also long-term care
You pay premiums	Low / no cost
No long-term care	Covers nursing homes

Coordinating Medicare as a Couple

Medicare is an *individual* program, not a household one. Each spouse enrolls based on their own age and work history, so the two of you can hit Medicare at different times. That alone surprises a lot of couples who'd assumed that they'd start together.

This matters most when one spouse keeps working while the other retires. As long as the working spouse stays on a solid employer plan, the covered spouse may be able to delay Medicare and avoid penalties, too. The key is confirming in writing that the employer plan counts as creditable coverage for both of you.

There's also a timing trap to consider. Smaller employers sometimes require Medicare to become your primary coverage at 65 even if you're still working. If that applies to either of you, delaying Medicare could leave a gap, but one quick call to the employer's benefits office can clear that up before a deadline sneaks past.

The practical move is to sit down together and put each spouse's 65th birthday on the same calendar. Decide who enrolls when, confirm whose plan covers whom, and keep the creditable coverage letters for both of you. Treat it like one shared plan even though the enrollments are separate, and you're far less likely to miss a window.

Quick Answers to Questions New Retirees Ask Most

Before you move ahead to Chapter 12, let's cover several quick but crucial FAQs that tend to come up at nearly every kitchen table.

Will Medicare pay for a nursing home? *Usually no. Medicare covers short rehab stays, not long-term custodial care. That cost falls to you, to long-term-care insurance, or eventually to Medicaid. Plan for it separately.*

Can I switch from Medicare Advantage back to Medigap later? *Sometimes, but not always easily. After your first window, a Medigap insurer can make you pass medical underwriting, so a health change could mean a higher premium or a denial. Choose your first path with that in mind.*

Does my coverage travel with me? *With Original Medicare plus Medigap, you can see any provider in the country that takes Medicare. Most Advantage plans tie you to a local network, so snowbirds and frequent travelers should check this before enrolling.*

Do I have to take Medicare at 65 if I'm on my spouse's employer plan? *Often no, as long as that plan counts as creditable coverage. Confirm it in writing, then use a Special Enrollment Period later to avoid the penalty.*

Do I sign up for Medicare automatically, or do I have to do it myself? *If you're already collecting Social Security, you're usually enrolled automatically at 65. If not, you have to sign up yourself, and missing that window is exactly where the late penalties begin.*

Does my spouse get Medicare through me? *No. Medicare is individual, not a household plan. Each spouse qualifies on their own work record and enrolls separately, even if only one of you worked.*

When can I change my plan if I picked the wrong one? *Each fall, during Medicare Open Enrollment from October 15 to December 7, you can switch plans for the following year. A choice that isn't working isn't locked in forever.*

CHAPTER 12:

THE MEDICARE SURCHARGE THAT CAN RAISE YOUR PREMIUMS

Most retirees assume that everyone pays the same price for Medicare, but they don't. A hidden rule ties your premium to your income, so a strong earning year, a property sale, a large withdrawal, or a Roth conversion can increase your Medicare premiums for the next two years.

When your income climbs above certain lines, your Medicare premium climbs too. Understand those lines now, and you can keep more of your check later.

The Medicare Premium Penalty Hidden in Higher Income

Retirement doesn't end the connection between your income and your healthcare costs. In fact, one can directly influence the other through the premiums you pay for Medicare.

Understanding IRMAA and Higher Medicare Premiums

The surcharge has a clunky name: the Income-Related Monthly Adjustment Amount, usually shortened to IRMAA. It's simply an extra charge added to your Medicare premiums when your income is higher than average.

Many of us picture Medicare premiums as a fixed cost, the same for every retiree in the program. So when a letter shows up announcing a higher premium because of income, it feels like a fee that's appeared out of nowhere.

The connection is the one we keep coming back to in this guide: Your income and your Medicare premium are tied together. The more income you report, the more you may pay for the very coverage pulled from your Social Security check. That's the same thread linking your withdrawals, your taxes, and now your healthcare costs. This should change how you think about every income decision in retirement. Remember, a withdrawal is rarely just a withdrawal, because it can nudge your taxes, your benefit taxation, and your Medicare premium all at once. Once you see those links, you stop making money moves in isolation and start thinking about how each one ripples across your whole picture.

The Income Thresholds That Trigger Higher Medicare Costs

So how does IRMAA work? It runs on income brackets, a bit like a staircase. As long as your income stays below the first step, you pay the standard premium. Step onto a higher one, and a surcharge gets added to both your Part B and Part D premiums.

The surcharge grows as you climb. A modest jump over the first line adds a smaller surcharge. Higher income puts you on higher steps, each with a larger amount tacked onto your monthly premiums. The brackets and dollar figures are adjusted over time, which means that the exact numbers shift from year to year.

However, IRMAA works like a cliff, not a ramp. If you land just one dollar over a bracket line, you pay the *full* surcharge for that entire step, not a small slice of it. That's very different from how income tax brackets work, in which only the dollars above each line are taxed at the higher rate. With IRMAA, crossing the line by a little costs the same as crossing it by a lot.

Because those figures change, confirm the current brackets at Medicare.gov. The Centers for Medicare & Medicaid Services publishes the current Part B and Part D figures each year, and the Social Security Administration explains the income rules in its guide for higher-income beneficiaries, SSA Publication No. 05-10536. Treat the brackets as lines that shift a little each year rather than permanent marks.

When Higher Income Triggers Higher Medicare Premiums

Many retirees come to see IRMAA as an extra tax on success, and that reaction makes sense. You worked hard, saved well, and now one strong income year raises your healthcare costs. It can feel like a penalty for doing things right.

Walter is a single retiree who usually keeps his income comfortably below the first IRMAA line. One year, he sells an investment property and pockets a large gain. That transaction lifts his income onto a higher step, and a surcharge gets added to his Medicare premiums.

Ray and Eileen, a married couple, convert a large chunk of a traditional IRA to a Roth in one year. The conversion counts as income, pushes them into a higher bracket, and raises their premiums too.

In both cases, these households made a big income move without realizing that it would ripple into their Medicare costs.

IRMAA: Monthly Part B by Income (2026)

Higher income can increase your monthly Medicare Part B premium.

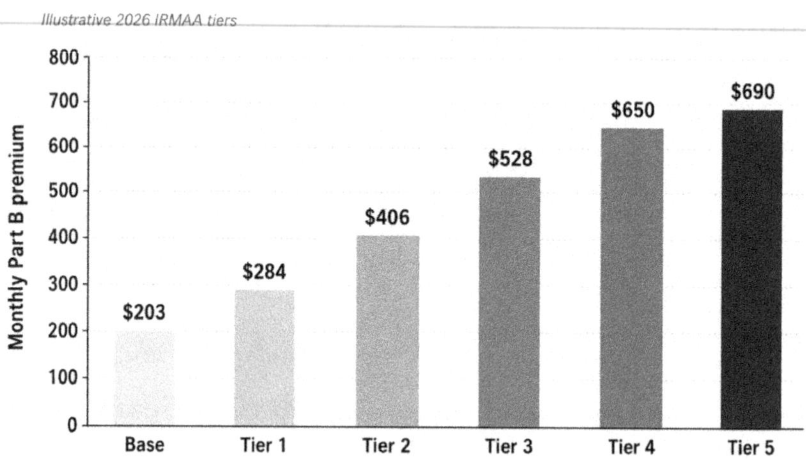

The surcharge, though, is usually temporary. IRMAA is tied to one year's income, so a single high-income year affects one year of premiums, then usually falls away once income returns to its normal level. Don't look at this as a permanent feature of retirement, because it's actually a one-time bump tied to a one-time event.

Before any large income event such as a property sale, a big withdrawal, or a sizable Roth conversion, pause and ask whether it could push you onto a higher IRMAA step.

Understanding IRMAA Timing Rules

IRMAA has a few quirks that catch people by surprise, mostly around timing. Once you understand them, you can stop worrying and start planning ahead.

The 2-Year Lookback Rule That Still Counts Old Income

Medicare doesn't look at your current income to set your premium. It looks back about two years to decide what you pay today.

In other words, the tax return from two years ago is what Medicare uses to set this year's premium. So a strong income year, even one well in the past, can raise your premium long after the money came and went.

This matters most in the years right around retirement. Your final working year, with its full salary, might be the very year Medicare looks at when it sets your premium two years later. That's why a brand-new retiree sometimes opens a letter announcing a surcharge based on income they no longer earn. Medicare is reading a snapshot of your income from two years back, then asking you to pay based on that older picture. Once you understand the lag, it becomes a predictable part of the system that you can plan around.

Retirement Doesn't Automatically Lower Your Medicare Premium

Many assume that when they stop working and their income drops, their Medicare premium drops right away. But because of the two-year lookback, it usually doesn't happen automatically.

Your income may have fallen the moment you retired, but Medicare is still looking at the higher figure from your working years. The system catches up eventually, just not right away.

But you do not have to sit and wait for that catch-up if a major life change has cut your income, because there's a way to tell Medicare that your situation has changed.

The Life Events That Can Lower Your Medicare Premium

Medicare allows you to ask for a lower premium when certain life events reduce your income. You file an appeal, explain the change, and Medicare can use your more recent, lower income instead of the older figure. There are several common events that qualify for this kind of adjustment.

- **Retirement:** Stopping work or cutting back to part-time often drops your income sharply
- **Loss of income:** A pension that ends or income property that stops paying can lower what you bring in
- **Divorce:** A change in marital status can change the income figure Medicare uses
- **Death of a spouse:** This often reduces household income and can shift your premium

The appeals process is more approachable than it sounds. You complete a form explaining the life event, provide some documentation, and ask Medicare to use your current income instead of the two-year-old figure. If you recently retired and a surcharge shows up based on your old salary, this is exactly the path to fix it.

So if a major life event has lowered your income, don't just accept a surcharge built on old numbers. Contact Social Security, ask about the IRMAA appeal, and request that they use your updated income. The form for this is Form SSA-44, the Social Security Administration's Medicare Income-Related Monthly Adjustment Amount Life-Changing Event form, and it exists for exactly this reason.

You note the life-changing event, estimate your reduced income, and attach a document or two that backs up your story, such as a letter from a former employer or proof of your retirement date. If your income has genuinely dropped, this is one of the friendlier pieces of paperwork in the whole system, because it's designed to give money *back* rather than take it away.

Healthcare Costs Before Medicare Eligibility

If you're thinking about retiring before 65, remember that Medicare doesn't begin until 65, so anyone who steps away earlier has to bridge that gap on their own. But with a little planning, it's easily manageable.

Covering the Years Before Medicare

You need health coverage during the years between your last day of work and your 65th birthday, but Medicare isn't yet an option. This is the coverage gap, and it's one of the biggest costs that early retirees fail to plan for.

The challenge often gets tangled up with the income decisions we've been outlining. To fund those early years, many retirees pull from a traditional IRA or convert savings to a Roth. Both moves count as income, and that income can do two things at once: raise the cost of your coverage today and set up an IRMAA surcharge two years down the road.

The consequence is that a withdrawal meant to cover living expenses can raise your healthcare costs from both directions. There's an easy way to keep this top of mind. In the years before 65, reporting more income can shrink the help you get on a marketplace plan today. In the years after, that same income can trigger an IRMAA surcharge two years later. So the dollars you pull out during early retirement can cost you twice: once now and once later. None of this means that you should avoid withdrawals or conversions. It just means that the timing and size are worth some thought before you act.

The Insurance Options Available Before Medicare Eligibility

You have several ways to stay covered until Medicare begins, and each one fits a different situation.

COBRA: *This lets you keep your former employer's health plan for a limited time after you leave. The coverage feels familiar but you pay the full premium yourself, so it often costs more than it did while you were working.*

ACA marketplace plans: *These are the plans you shop for on the health insurance marketplace. Your premium depends on your income, and a lower reported income can mean meaningful subsidies, which ties right back to how you draw down your savings.*

Employer coverage options: *Some employers offer retiree health benefits, and a working spouse's plan can sometimes cover you too. These are worth checking first, since they may be the simplest and most affordable route.*

Always look beyond the monthly premium. Deductibles, out-of-pocket limits, and which doctors are covered all shape what you actually pay over a year.

Building Healthcare Costs Into an Early Retirement Plan

The simplest way to avoid a surprise is to give healthcare its own line in your retirement budget. Treat it as a real, recurring expense like housing or food for every year between your retirement date and 65.

A little coordination here prevents income-related surprises. Because the income you report affects both your ACA subsidy now and your IRMAA surcharge later, the timing of your withdrawals and Roth conversions matters. Spreading large income moves across several years, instead of cramming them into one, can keep both costs lower.

If you plan to retire before 65, map out how you'll stay covered and what it'll cost before you hand in your notice. That way, the coverage gap becomes a planned part of retirement instead of an expensive surprise.

PART IV

WRAP-UP

You've now worked through the fourth and final question in the Money Code Framework: *How do Medicare decisions affect my retirement income*? Before we fully tie things up, let's pull together the key points.

The Core Ideas

The Medicare decisions you make at 65 can shape your spendable income for years. IRMAA can raise your healthcare costs after a strong income year, often two years later than expected. And healthcare planning belongs inside your retirement-income plan, right alongside claiming and taxes.

Common Medicare Mistakes

Keep an eye on the traps that catch people most often:

- Missing an enrollment deadline and locking in a lifelong penalty
- Ignoring IRMAA exposure before a large income event
- Confusing Medicare and Medicaid when long-term care comes up

Your Final Money Code Action Plan

The final steps that bring everything together:

1. Identify your Medicare enrollment timeline and mark the windows
2. Review whether future income events could trigger an IRMAA surcharge
3. Compare your Medicare coverage options
4. Schedule your annual retirement-income review

With all four corners in place, you have something that most retirees never build: one coordinated plan. Our final chapter brings the entire Money Code Framework together and shows how it all fits into a clear, one-page plan before you ever file a claim or enroll in Medicare. What's more, it'll show you what that confidence means when you move from learning the rules to actually putting them into practice.

YOUR MONEY, YOUR MOVE:

THE MONEY CODE FRAMEWORK IN ACTION

You opened this book with a worry that follows millions of people into retirement, the feeling of having so many unanswered questions about the money you spent a lifetime earning. That worry should be much smaller now, because page by page within this book, you've taken control of your knowledge.

The Key Decisions Behind Your Plan

The first decision of when to claim sets the size of every check you'll ever receive, and the right age for *you* is the one that fits your health, your savings, and the people who depend on you. By now you can pull your real numbers instead of guessing, read your own statement, and run a break-even comparison before you file rather than after.

For a married couple, the picture widens. A household has one income to protect, not two separate checks, and the higher earner's timing sets the floor for whoever lives longer. Along the way you encountered the spousal benefit, the divorced-spouse benefit that can outlast a marriage by decades, and the survivor strategy of drawing one check now and switching to the larger one later. And working in retirement, it turns out, rarely costs you benefits for good, because what the earnings test holds onto is only temporary, and it all comes back to you.

What You Get to Keep

Collecting your benefits and keeping them are separate things altogether. You can now see how your combined income decides whether the tax man takes a share of your check, how the order you draw from your accounts can either raise or lower that bill, and how a few well-timed Roth conversions in your quieter years can lighten the load for the rest of retirement.

Medicare turns out to be as much a money decision as a health one, since its premiums come straight out of your Social Security check. You can spot the enrollment windows that carry lifelong penalties, weigh the real difference between Medigap and Medicare Advantage, and watch for the income surcharge called IRMAA that can raise your premiums two years after a single strong income year.

Why It All Connects

All of this became easy to understand once someone laid it out in plain language. The hard part was seeing how all the rules connect, and that's exactly what you can now do. It's become clear that a withdrawal is rarely just a withdrawal, and that a claiming choice ripples into your taxes and your Medicare premium. The wisest decisions come from seeing the whole picture before you touch any single piece of it, and that's the real advantage this book has given you.

Your Money Code Action Plan

Knowing the rules is essential, but then you have to actually do something with them. Below, we've condensed everything this book advised you to do, gathered into one concise plan. Work through it in order and you'll have made every decision that matters before you ever sign a form.

Step 1: Lock In Your Claiming Age

Start with your real numbers, because every other decision rests on them, then choose your timing intentionally.

1. Create or log in to your account at ssa.gov and write down your estimated benefit at 62, at your Full Retirement Age, and at 70
2. Check your earnings record for missing or unusually low years. If you or your spouse earned a public-sector pension, confirm how the 2025 repeal of WEP and GPO affects your benefit
3. Calculate your break-even age, and weigh it honestly against your health and your family's longevity
4. Pick a tentative claiming age, and write something brief about why it fits your life

Step 2: Coordinate Your Household Benefits

If anyone else's income is tied to yours, plan as one household rather than two.

1. If you're married, compare both estimates side by side and decide who files first. In most cases, the higher earner should wait because that check becomes the survivor's protection
2. Check whether a spousal benefit, up to half of your spouse's full amount, beats your own
3. If you were married for at least 10 years and are now single, compare a benefit on your former spouse's record. They're never notified, and their check is untouched
4. If you've lost a spouse, compare the survivor benefit with your own, and consider claiming one now and switching to the larger one later
5. If you plan to work before your FRA, estimate your earnings against the annual limit so that a temporary reduction doesn't catch you off guard.

Step 3: Protect What You Keep from Taxes

Remember, what you collect and what you keep aren't the same number, and a little planning protects the difference.

1. Estimate your combined income and whether it pushes part of your benefit into the taxable range
2. Set a withdrawal order. Drawing from taxable accounts first and Roth accounts last is a sensible starting point
3. Hunt for low-income years, often early in retirement when a modest Roth conversion can lower your taxes for good, and plan ahead for required minimum distributions, which generally begin at 73

Step 4: Get Your Medicare Decisions Right

Medicare costs follow you for life, so the choices around age 65 deserve your attention.

1. Mark your enrollment window around your 65th birthday. If you delay because of employer coverage, keep written proof that the coverage is creditable
2. Decide between Original Medicare with a Medigap policy and a Medicare Advantage plan, based on your actual healthcare needs and how much you travel
3. Before any large income event such as a property sale, a big withdrawal, or a sizable Roth conversion, check whether it could trigger an IRMAA surcharge two years later

Your One-Page Money Code Blueprint

When you've worked through those steps, boil the result down to just five lines. Keep it to one single page so that you can keep it in a drawer, a folder, or a note on your phone.

Claiming age: The age you intend to file, and a short note on why

Household strategy: Who files first, who waits, and which spousal, divorced-spouse, or survivor benefits you're coordinating

Tax strategy: Your withdrawal order and any Roth conversions that you're timing

Medicare strategy: Your enrollment dates, your coverage path, and your IRMAA watch points

Annual review date: The one day a year you check all of it

Keep that page where you'll be able to access it easily and revisit it once a year on a birthday or at tax time, updating your figures from ssa.gov, medicare.gov, and irs.gov.

The ultimate advantage here is knowing the rules before you choose, and this book has provided them for you with no fuss or complicated jargon. So decide on facts instead of fear, act before you file rather than after, and then you'll be able to walk in as the most prepared person at the table.

Because the smartest retirement decision is the one you make *before* you're forced to make it.

SOCIAL SECURITY & MEDICARE REFERENCE TOOLKIT

This reference section is for the day you sit down to act, when you want a quick primer instead of a full reread. Keep these pages close, because they turn what you've learned into something you can use in a single sitting.

Current-Year Update Method

The most useful habit to adopt here is to check the current figures before you decide anything. The rules behind Social Security and Medicare stay generally steady, but the numbers tied to them move a little each year.

So make this your first step every time: Before any major decision, pull the current numbers from the official sources. It takes only a few minutes and it keeps your whole plan honest.

This matters most when you hear someone saying that Social Security is running out of money. Usually, they mean that the program's reserve funds could run low in the years ahead. In practical terms, even if those reserves are depleted, payroll taxes from current workers would still be coming in and are projected to cover a large majority of scheduled benefits. Insolvency would mean a possible future reduction rather than a disappearance, so your decisions should rest on current law. If you want to track any changes, check the official sources below instead of what they're saying on the news.

Bookmark these so that the update takes seconds:

Topic	Verify Current Figure At
Full Retirement Age	SSA.gov
Earnings Test Limit	SSA.gov
Taxable Benefits Thresholds	IRS.gov
Medicare Premiums	Medicare.gov
IRMAA Brackets	Medicare.gov
Part B Premium	Medicare.gov

WHAT TO READ NEXT

If you're compelled to go deeper, we offer two additional books that pick up where this one ends.

For readers looking to connect their trust to the bigger financial picture:

Living Trusts + Wills, Retirement, Tax & Estate Planning: The 6-in-1 Guide covers retirement planning, tax strategy, and generational wealth.

Grab it here: **urlgeni.us/amazon/generationalwealth**

For readers navigating the concerns that accompany aging:

Living Trusts, Wills & Estate Planning for Seniors covers Medicaid eligibility, long-term care, and late-stage asset protection.

Grab it here: **urlgeni.us/amazon/trustsforseniors**

THE SOCIAL SECURITY ACTION PACK

Because you've made it all the way to the end, you've earned access to **10 FREE companion resources** designed to help you put what you've learned into action and make more confident Social Security and Medicare decisions.

Here's what you'll get:

1. The Social Security Money Code Action Pack
2. Interactive Claiming Age Calculator
3. 10-Year Retirement Roadmap
4. Major Life Change Planning Checklist
5. Social Security & Medicare Quick Reference Guide
6. 12-Month Pre-Claiming Countdown
7. "Call SSA Like A Pro" Script Pack
8. Tax-Free Retirement Paycheck Blueprint
9. Free Government Benefits Beyond Social Security
10. Widow(er) First-90-Days Action Card

To download your bonuses, scan the QR code or go to:

MonroeMethod.com/social-security

Download Here

IF THIS BOOK HELPED YOU...

Thanks for reading our book.

We invested significant time working with experienced professionals, including retirement tax specialists, financial planning experts, and healthcare and Medicare reviewers, to ensure this book provides accurate, practical, and easy-to-understand guidance on some of the most important retirement decisions you'll ever make.

Our goal was to make reliable Social Security and Medicare information accessible to everyone, without requiring costly consultations just to understand the basics or avoid common mistakes.

If this book has helped you feel more informed and confident about your retirement planning, we'd be incredibly grateful if you took a moment to leave a short review on Amazon. Every review helps other readers discover the book, and we truly appreciate your support.

To leave a review scan the QR code or go to:

mybook.to/social-security

GLOSSARY

A few terms come up repeatedly in retirement planning, so we've compiled them below in plain language so that a lack of clarity never gets between you and a clear decision.

Break-even age: The age at which the total money from waiting to claim catches up to the total money from claiming early.

COLA (cost-of-living adjustment): The yearly increase that raises your benefit to help it keep pace with rising prices. It's one reason that a larger starting check can grow into an even larger one over time.

Creditable coverage: Health or drug coverage that Medicare considers at least as good as its own, which lets you delay enrollment without a late penalty.

Deemed filing: A rule meaning that when you apply, Social Security treats you as claiming everything you're eligible for at that moment. That's why most old "claim one, switch later" strategies no longer work.

Delayed retirement credits: The increase your benefit earns for each month you wait past Full Retirement Age, up to age 70, worth roughly 8% per year.

Divorced-spouse benefit: A benefit you may claim on a former spouse's record if the marriage lasted at least 10 years and you're not currently remarried.

Earnings test: The rule that temporarily withholds part of your benefit if you claim before Full Retirement Age and earn above an annual limit. The withheld money is credited back later.

FRA (Full Retirement Age): The age the system treats as your baseline, when you receive your full calculated benefit with no early reduction and no delayed bonus. For most people approaching retirement, it falls between 66 and 67.

GPO (Government Pension Offset): A rule that, until it was repealed by the Social Security Fairness Act in 2025, reduced the spousal or survivor benefit of someone who also earned a pension from certain jobs that didn't pay Social Security taxes. It no longer applies.

Initial and Special Enrollment Periods: Your first seven-month window to sign up for Medicare around age 65, and the later penalty-free window available if you kept creditable employer coverage.

IRMAA (Income-Related Monthly Adjustment Amount): An extra charge added to your Medicare premiums when your income climbs above certain lines. Think of it as a surcharge that kicks in like a staircase, one full step at a time.

Medicare Advantage (Part C): An all-in-one alternative to Original Medicare offered by private insurers, usually with its own provider network.

Medigap: Private Medicare Supplement insurance that pairs with Original Medicare to cover the deductibles and cost-sharing it leaves to you.

Primary Insurance Amount (PIA): Your baseline benefit, the amount you'd receive at your Full Retirement Age. Spousal and survivor benefits are measured against this figure.

Provisional income (aka combined income): The measure the IRS uses to decide how much of your benefit is taxed. You add your regular taxable income, any tax-free interest, and half of your Social Security benefit.

Required Minimum Distribution (RMD): The amount the IRS requires you to withdraw each year from traditional retirement accounts, generally starting at age 73.

Roth conversion: Moving money from a traditional IRA into a Roth IRA, paying tax now so that the money grows and comes out tax-free later.

Spousal benefit: A benefit that a lower-earning spouse can claim on the higher earner's record, worth up to 50% of that spouse's full benefit.

Survivor benefits: The benefit that lets a surviving spouse keep the larger of the household's two checks after one partner dies.

WEP (Windfall Elimination Provision): A rule that, until it was repealed by the Social Security Fairness Act in 2025, reduced the Social Security benefit of someone who also earned a pension from work where they did not pay Social Security taxes, such as certain government jobs. It no longer applies.

Keep in mind that this guide is for educational purposes only, and it's not personal financial, tax, or legal advice. Program rules and figures change over time. Confirm current details with the Social Security Administration, Medicare, the IRS, or a qualified professional before making any decision specific to your situation.

SOURCES

1. Board of Trustees, Federal Old-Age and Survivors Insurance and Federal Disability Insurance Trust Funds, *The 2025 Annual Report of the Board of Trustees of the Federal Old-Age and Survivors Insurance and Federal Disability Insurance Trust Funds* (Washington, DC: U.S. Government Publishing Office, 2025), https://www.ssa.gov/oact/tr.

2. Centers for Medicare & Medicaid Services. *Enrollment Periods*. Medicare.gov. https://www.medicare.gov/basics/get-started-with-medicare/sign-up/when-can-i-sign-up-for-medicare.

3. Centers for Medicare & Medicaid Services. *Learn How Medigap Works*. Medicare.gov. https://www.medicare.gov/health-drug-plans/medigap/basics/how-medigap-works.

4. Centers for Medicare & Medicaid Services. *Medicare and Medicaid*. Medicare.gov. https://www.medicare.gov/basics/costs/help/medicaid.

5. Centers for Medicare & Medicaid Services. *Medicare Costs*. Medicare.gov. https://www.medicare.gov/basics/costs/medicare-costs.

6. Centers for Medicare & Medicaid Services. *Monthly Premium for Drug Plans*. Medicare.gov. https://www.medicare.gov/basics/costs/medicare-costs/part-d-costs.

7. Centers for Medicare & Medicaid Services. *Part B Costs*. Medicare.gov. https://www.medicare.gov/basics/costs/medicare-costs.

8. Centers for Medicare & Medicaid Services. *Part B Late Enrollment Penalty*. Medicare.gov. https://www.medicare.gov/basics/costs/medicare-costs/avoid-penalties.

9. Centers for Medicare & Medicaid Services. *Part D Late Enrollment Penalty*. Medicare.gov. https://www.medicare.gov/basics/costs/medicare-costs/avoid-penalties.

10. Centers for Medicare & Medicaid Services. *What's Not Covered by Part A & Part B?* Medicare.gov. https://www.medicare.gov/providers-services/original-medicare/not-covered.

11. Centers for Medicare & Medicaid Services. *When Does Medicare Coverage Start?* Medicare.gov. https://www.medicare.gov/basics/get-started-with-medicare/sign-up/when-does-medicare-coverage-start.

12. Internal Revenue Service. *Instructions for Form 1040 and 1040-SR: Social Security Benefits Worksheet.* U.S. Department of the Treasury, Internal Revenue Service. https://www.irs.gov/forms-instructions.

13. Internal Revenue Service. *Publication 590-B: Distributions from Individual Retirement Arrangements (IRAs)*. U.S. Department of the Treasury, Internal Revenue Service. https://www.irs.gov/forms-pubs/about-publication-590-b.

14. Internal Revenue Service. *Publication 915: Social Security and Equivalent Railroad Retirement Benefits*. U.S. Department of the Treasury, Internal Revenue Service. https://www.irs.gov/forms-pubs/about-publication-915.

15. Internal Revenue Service. *Retirement Topics: Required Minimum Distributions (RMDs)*. U.S. Department of the Treasury, Internal Revenue Service. https://www.irs.gov/retirement-plans/retirement-plans-faqs-regarding-required-minimum-distributions.

16. Internal Revenue Service. *Roth IRAs*. U.S. Department of the Treasury, Internal Revenue Service. https://www.irs.gov/retirement-plans/roth-iras.

17. Social Security Administration. *Benefits for Your Family: Divorced Spouse*. U.S. Social Security Administration. https://www.ssa.gov.

18. Social Security Administration, *Delayed Retirement Credits*, U.S. Social Security Administration, accessed June 15, 2026, https://www.ssa.gov/benefits/retirement/planner/delayret.html.

19. Social Security Administration. *Full Retirement Age*. U.S. Social Security Administration. https://www.ssa.gov/benefits/retirement/planner/ageincrease.html.

20. Social Security Administration. *If You Are Divorced*. U.S. Social Security Administration. https://www.ssa.gov.

21. Social Security Administration. *If You Are the Survivor*. U.S. Social Security Administration. Accessed June 15, 2026. https://www.ssa.gov/benefits/survivors/ifyou.html.

22. Social Security Administration, *If You Change Your Mind (Form SSA-521: Request for Withdrawal of Application)*, U.S. Social Security Administration, accessed June 15, 2026, https://www.ssa.gov/benefits/retirement/planner/withdrawal.html.

23. Social Security Administration. *Income Taxes and Your Social Security Benefits*. U.S. Social Security Administration. https://www.ssa.gov/benefits/retirement/planner/taxes.html.

24. Social Security Administration. *Medicare Income-Related Monthly Adjustment Amount—Life-Changing Event (Form SSA-44)*. U.S. Social Security Administration. https://www.ssa.gov/forms/ssa-44.pdf.

25. Social Security Administration. *Medicare Premiums: Rules for Higher-Income Beneficiaries* (SSA Publication No. 05-10536). U.S. Social Security Administration. https://www.ssa.gov/pubs/EN-05-10536.pdf.

26. Social Security Administration. *Receiving Benefits While Working*. U.S. Social Security Administration. https://www.ssa.gov/benefits/retirement/planner/whileworking.html.

27. Social Security Administration. *Retirement Benefits*. U.S. Social Security Administration. https://www.ssa.gov/benefits/retirement/.

28. Social Security Administration, *Survivors Benefits*, U.S. Social Security Administration, accessed June 15, 2026, https://www.ssa.gov/benefits/survivors/.

29. Social Security Administration, *Understanding the Benefits* (Baltimore, MD: U.S. Social Security Administration, n.d.), https://www.ssa.gov/pubs/EN-05-10024.pdf.

30. Social Security Board of Trustees. *The 2023 Annual Report of the Board of Trustees of the Federal Old-Age and Survivors Insurance and Federal Disability Insurance Trust Funds*. U.S. Social Security Administration. https://www.ssa.gov/oact/tr/2023/.

www.ingramcontent.com/pod-product-compliance
Lightning Source LLC
LaVergne TN
LVHW021131300926
849160LV00010B/957
9798993878737